Selected Praise fo.

Body Work

"Melissa Febos has written one of the most liberating books on the subject of writing that I can think of. A tender, urgent intelligence, a wisdom that is hard-won, and a rigor born from a love for the craft preside . . . I learned so much reading *Body Work* that I can't wait to teach and use on the page."   —ALEXANDER CHEE, author of *How to Write an Autobiographical Novel*

"Ferociously smart and piercingly insightful, *Body Work* is an instant classic of the how-and-why-do-we-write form. With candor and clarity, Melissa Febos explores the complexities of writing courageously and honestly about our lives. It's a book I'll return to again and again."
—CHERYL STRAYED, author of *Wild*

"Melissa Febos's *Body Work* is the most necessary book about memoir I've read. Daring, honest, psychologically insightful, and absolutely whip smart. A must-read for anybody shoving a pen across paper or staring into a screen or a past."   —MARY KARR, author of *The Art of Memoir*

Girlhood

"Febos proves herself to be one of the great documenters of the terrible and exquisite depths of girlhood. These essays are moss and iron—hard and beautiful—and struck through with Febos's signature brilliance and power and grace. An essential, heartbreaking project."

—CARMEN MARIA MACHADO,
author of *In the Dream House*

"Between the intellect and the body a third term emerges, dissolving binaries and reinventing the space of erotic power and creativity. A fuck-all guide to resilience and reclamation, a breathtaking reimagination of who we might be in spite of what we've been told. *Girlhood* will bring you back to life." —LIDIA YUKNAVITCH,
author of *The Chronology of Water*

"An exquisite collection. Febos's insight is devastating, the examinations of her world—from the female body, queerness, consent, slut-shaming, and intimacy—are rigorous and compassionate." —STEPHANIE DANLER,
author of *Sweetbitter*

"Febos is an intoxicating writer, but I found myself most grateful for the vivid clarity of her thinking . . . disquisitive and catalytic—it doesn't demand change so much as expose certain injustices so starkly that you might feel you cannot abide them another minute." —*The Atlantic*

"Febos's own voice is so irreverent and original . . . in a feminist canon that includes Adrienne Rich, and Maggie Nelson's theory-minded masterpieces: smart, radical company." —*The New York Times Book Review*

"Febos illuminates how women are conditioned to be complicit in our own exploitation. Like much of her scholarship, it begins with somatic knowledge of the self." —*The Washington Post*

Abandon Me

"Febos is a strikingly talented writer who pushes at the boundaries of her form and shows us just how amazing and expansive it can be." —JENNY OFFILL, author of *Dept. of Speculation*

"It's rare to read a book as generous as it is genius . . . I don't know that I've ever felt more thankful to read a book." —KIESE LAYMON, author of *Heavy*

"Bold . . . Mesmerizing . . . The sheer fearlessness of the narrative is captivating." —*The New Yorker*

"Anyone who's read Febos . . . knows that her work explores boundaries as deftly as it defies categorization."

—*Esquire*

Body Work

Body Work

The Radical Power of Personal Narrative

✦

MELISSA FEBOS

Catapult
New York

ISBN: 978-1-64622-085-4

Cover design by Nicole Caputo
Book design by Wah-Ming Chang

Library of Congress Control Number: 2021941016

Catapult
New York, NY
books.catapult.co

Printed in the United States of America
3 5 7 9 10 8 6 4 2

For my students

Contents

Author's Note

This is not a craft book in the traditional sense. That is, this book is not a manifesto or a manual. There are many great volumes of such books and I've listed some of them in my bibliography. While there is some practical advice herein, that is not the aim of this book. These essays are attempts to describe the ways that writing is integrated into the fundamental movements of my life: political, corporeal, spiritual, psychological, and social. They are by no means comprehensive even in this task.

I have found that a fulfilling writing life is one in which the creative process merges with the other necessary processes of good living, which only the individual can define. This holistic approach is pragmatic in the sense that it ensures the discipline, because while I some-times resist the work of writing, I resist my own psychic suffering more, and writing has become for me a primary means of digesting and integrating my experiences and thereby reducing the pains of living, or if not, at least making them useful to myself and to others. There is no pain in my life that has not been given value by the al-chemy of creative attention.

Cultivating this kind of relationship to writing has also, to a great extent, relieved me from the bondage of my own vanities, which pose a greater threat to my creative practice than any other constraint, including that of time. I have observed that we bring the best of ourselves to writing and that publishing brings out our worst. I like to think that my relationship to making art is utterly discrete from my relationship to reception, the latter being ambivalent at best. I am immeasurably grateful for the privilege of publication and I also know that seeking self-esteem in its rewards is a dicey enter-prise, at least for those of us who cherish our mental serenity and want to preserve the pleasurable aspects of creation.

I became a writer because I loved writing and I still

do. I became a writer because the process helped me survive and it still does. I do not think that the vocation of writer is superior to any other, but I do believe it is the most useful life for me, the one in which I can most be of service to this questionable project of human civilization—partly because it is where my strengths lie, and partly because it keeps me stable enough to be available in other respects.

I did not interview other writers for the purposes of this book, though the idea tempted me. There are an infinite number of people whose experiences would differently illustrate the principles I've set down, but here I have focused on articulating my own thoughts. This is appropriate, I suppose, for a book about devotion to the practice of personal writing.

For reasons that I delineate in the following pages, many writers and potential writers have been discouraged from this practice. I hope that this book also provides a counterpoint to some of the arguments that lurk behind such discouragement, and to make transparent their fundamental superficiality and some of their many implicit biases. Writing is a form of freedom more accessible than many and there are forces at work that would like to withhold it from those whose stories most threaten the regimes that govern this society. Fuck them. Write your life. Let this book be a totem of permission, encouragement, proof, whatever you need it to be.

Melissa Febos
April 2021
Iowa City, IA

Body Work

I

In Praise of Navel-Gazing

In a recent nonfiction workshop I taught, a female student cringed when I suggested she include more of her own story in an essay. The narrative experimented with form, and suggested a history of sexual trauma, but quickly shifted into more lyrical and analytical musing on the general subject. She frowned. "But I don't want to seem self-absorbed. You know, *navel-gazing*." The rest of the room—nearly all women—nodded. This is a scene that has played out everywhere I have taught writing: at colleges of all sizes, conferences, and private salons. It is a concern I have heard from countless students and peers,

and which I have often greeted with a combination of baf-
flement and frustration. Since when did telling our own
stories and deriving their insights become so reviled? It
doesn't matter if the story is your own, I tell them over and
over, only that you tell it well. Should we not always tell
stories so that their specificity reveals some larger truth?

And yet. How many times have I been privy to conversations among other writers in which we sneer at the
very concept? We compulsively assure each other that
writing isn't about enacting a kind of *therapy*. How gross!
We are intellectuals. We are artists. "I mean, you can't
expect people to be interested in your *diary*," a friend and
fellow teacher exclaimed once. I nodded. What kind of
monstrous narcissist would make that mistake?

I am complicit. I have committed this betrayal of my
own experience innumerable times. But I am done agree-
ing when my peers spit on the idea of writing as transformation, as catharsis, as—dare I say it—therapy. Tell me:
who is writing in their therapeutic diary and then dash-
ing it off to be published? I don't know who these supposedly self-indulgent (and extravagantly well-connected)
narcissists are. But I suspect that when people denigrate
them in the abstract, they are picturing women. I'm finished referring, in a derogatory way, to stories of body

and sex and gender and violence and joy and childhood
and family as *navel-gazing*.

A few years ago at a writers' conference, during a
panel of literary magazine editors, a female audience
member posed a question about the potential audience
for her story of surviving a familiar kind of trauma.
One of the male editors on the panel rolled his eyes and
shrugged. "I mean, I'm not sure we need any more of
those stories." The other panelists nodded in consensus:
Stories like hers belonged on talk shows, not in the hal-
lowed realm of literary prose. Everyone knows we don't
need another one of those. The genre of victimhood is
already so crowded. So gauche.

Later that day, while serving on a panel of memoirists, I polled the audience—a room packed with a few
hundred readers and writers. I asked for a show of hands:
"Who here has experienced an act of violence, abuse, ex-
treme disempowerment, sexual aggression, harassment,
or humiliation?" The room fell silent as the air filled with
hands.

In response to a surge of popular memoirs, William H.
Gass, in a 1994 issue of *Harper's Magazine*, asked, "Are

there any motives for the enterprise that aren't tainted with conceit or a desire for revenge or a wish for justification? To halo a sinner's head? To puff an ego already inflated past safety?" He went on: "To have written an autobiography is already to have made yourself a monster . . . Why is it so exciting to say, now that everyone knows it anyway, 'I was born . . . I was born . . . I was born'? 'I pooped in my pants, I was betrayed, I made straight A's.'" It is an argument that has been made for centuries, and that I have heard all my writing life.

It is the reason that I did not want to write a memoir. At twenty-six, I was an MFA student in fiction, deep into what I believed was a Very Important Novel about addiction and female sexuality. Then I took a nonfiction craft class for which we were asked to write a short memoir. Though the content of my novel drew heavily from my own experience, I had never written any kind of nonfiction. The twenty-page essay I drafted about my years as a professional dominatrix was the most urgent thing I had ever written. When he read it, my professor insisted that I drop whatever I was working on and write a memoir.

I cringed. Who was I, a twenty-six-year-old woman, a former junky and sex worker, to presume that strangers should find my life interesting? I had already learned that

there were few more damning presumptions than that of
a young woman thinking her own story might be meaningful. Besides, I was writing a Very Important Novel.

"No way," I told my professor. I was determined to
stick to my more humble presumption that strangers
might be interested in a story *made up* by a twenty-six-
year-old former junky sex worker.

Do you see how easy it is to poke holes in this logic?

But my own story wouldn't leave me alone. It called
to me the way I have since come to recognize is the call
of my best stories, the ones that most need to be told.
So I wrote it. And it was urgent, but not easy. In order
to write that book, I had to walk back through my most
mystifying choices and excavate events for which I had
been numb on the first go-around.

That book was about being a sex worker and recovering from heroin addiction. It was about desire, shame,
bodies, drugs, and money. It was an intellectual inquiry
into these topics as much as it was a psychological and
emotional reckoning. In hindsight, I can say that the
compulsion to write it was an expression of my need to
understand what the connections were between those
things. To answer my own questions about why I had
ended up shooting speedballs and spanking men for

a living, and how the power of secrecy could become a prison. I wrote it because I wanted to show the strangers who shared those experiences that they were not alone.

I didn't write a memoir to free myself, though in the process I did.

In the 1980s, social psychologist James W. Pennebaker conducted some now-famous studies on his theory of expressive writing. Pennebaker instructed participants in his experimental group to write about a past trauma, expressing their very deepest thoughts and feelings surrounding it. In contrast, control participants were asked to write as objectively and factually as possible about neutral topics without revealing their emotions or opinions. For both groups, the schedule was fifteen minutes of continuous writing repeated over four consecutive days.

Some of the participants in the experimental group found the exercise upsetting. All of them found it valuable and meaningful. Monitoring over the subsequent year revealed that those participants made significantly fewer visits to physicians. Pennebaker's research has since been replicated numerous times and his results supported: Expressive writing about trauma strengthens the immune system, decreases obsessive thinking, and contributes to the overall health of the writers. And this is after only *four days* of fifteen-minute sessions. Pennebaker has since written extensively about how this effect can also be consistent on a much larger scale, in communities who have suffered the atrocities of war and other political events. The articulation of painful memories, including the literature and art that arises out of political upheaval, is integral to the formation, preservation, and integration of collective memory.

Let's face it: if you write about your wounds, it is likely to be therapeutic. Of course, the writing done in those fifteen minutes was surely terrible by artistic standards. But it is a logical fallacy to conclude that *any* writing with therapeutic effect is terrible.

You don't have to be into therapy to be healed by writing. Being healed does not have to be your goal. But to oppose the very idea of it is nonsensical, unless you consider what such a bias reveals about our values as a culture. Knee-jerk bias backed by flimsy logic and pseudoscience has always been a preferred disguise of our national prejudices.

That these topics of the body, the emotional interior, the domestic, the sexual, and the relational are all undervalued in intellectual literary terms, and are all associated with the female spheres of being, is not a co-incidence. This bias against personal writing is often a sexist mechanism, founded on the false binary between the emotional (female) and the intellectual (male), and intended to subordinate the former.

That is, Karl Ove Knausgaard is a genius, a risk-taker for his chronicles of the interior and the domestic, while my female graduate students are terrified to write about being mothers for fear that they will be deemed (or already are) vacuous narcissists. Or, as Maggie Nelson, in *The Argonauts*, says of a man inquiring how she could possibly pen a book on the subject of cruelty while pregnant: "Leave it to the old patrician white guy to call the lady speaker back to her body, so that no one misses the spectacle of that wild oxymoron, the pregnant woman who thinks. Which is really just a pumped-up version of that more general oxymoron, a woman who thinks."

While I balked at the idea of writing a memoir as a graduate student, I also shied away from the idea of being a *political* writer. I had only a hazy idea of what the ideal profile for a political writer or their work should be, but it definitely included having strong and unchanging opinions about politics, and surely did not include accounts of the writer's most vulnerable corporeal experiences. Probably, I pictured a man. What I did not consider were any of the historical examples of politicized personal writing (is there any other kind?) that were often part of a long-standing tradition of testimony, much of which I'd read, like *Incidents in the Life of a Slave Girl*, *The Diary of a Young Girl*, *Red Azalea*, and *Night*. Not to mention the many politically powerful memoirs published more recently that I'd devoured. No, my resistance to and bias against memoir was not based in any lived experience as a writer or a reader. It was my own internalized sexism, calling from inside the house to warn me away from telling my own story, because doing so might free me from shame and replace the onus of change onto the society in which we live.

When I was in graduate school, Dian Million had not yet published her brilliant article, "Felt Theory: An Indigenous Feminist Approach to Affect and History," but I wish that I could go back in time and give it to myself. In it, she makes "the case for remembering and understanding the impact of Canadian First Nation women's first-person and experiential narrative on white, mostly male mainstream scholarship," and examines how the suppression of this *felt experience* has been a collaboration between colonization, racism, and sexism, which all understand the political power of such stories and their threat to existing colonial social structures. Million argues that "these narratives were political acts in themselves that in their time exploded the measured 'objective' accounts of Canadian (and U.S.) colonial histories . . . Native women's personal narrative explored the racialized, gendered, and sexual nature of their colonization. In doing so, they transformed the debilitating force of an old social control, *shame*, into a social change agent in their generation." When I read this for the first time, I understood in a new way that resistance to the lived stories of women, and those of all oppressed people, is a resistance to justice.

The history of trauma and its stories has always been politicized. Consider the case of hysteria, that mysterious illness that captivated male doctors from antiquity until the beginning of the twentieth century. First known as wandering womb, its cause was believed to be a rogue uterus, which the ancient Greek doctor Aretaeus poetically described as an "animal within an animal," who "delights also in fragrant smells, and advances towards them," as if the female reproductive anatomy were akin to an opossum rooting through the neighborhood trash cans.

Hysteria had wide-ranging symptoms—from failure to marry to deafness and vomiting—and afflicted mostly women, though in staggering numbers. Its treatments ranged from physician-administered masturbation with early vibrators, to "water treatments" at sanitariums frequented by the wealthy, to institutionalization. In the late nineteenth century, rivalries between psychoanalysts like Freud and Pierre Janet drove research of the affliction to unprecedented lengths. "For a brief decade," writes Judith Herman in *Trauma and Recovery*, "men of science listened to women with a devotion and a respect unparalleled before or since."

What those men determined was this: Hysteria was caused by traumatic events. The symptoms of hysteria were the result of intrusive traumatic memories. As Freud and Josef Breuer wrote: "Hysterics suffer mainly from reminiscences." They also determined that the symptoms of hysteria could be resolved when the stories of those traumatic memories were put into words.

Thus began the practice of modern psychotherapy, what the famous patient known pseudonymously as Anna O. called the talking cure.

Freud listened to his hysteric patients. What he repeatedly heard were accounts of sexual abuse, assault, and incest. Freud believed he had solved the mystery of hysteria. In his now-famous paper "The Aetiology of Hysteria," he shared "the thesis that at the bottom of every case of hysteria there are *one or more occurrences of premature sexual experience*, occurrences which belong to the earliest years of childhood." It was, and perhaps remains, his greatest, most groundbreaking work, and an indicator that the sexual abuse of girls was rampant, across every social class. Herman writes that "this paper still rivals contemporary clinical descriptions of the effects of childhood sexual abuse. It is a brilliant, compassionate, eloquently argued, closely reasoned document."

Instead of enjoying his anticipated professional triumph, Freud retracted his findings within a year of publishing them. He had neglected to consider the grave social implications of his revelation. If the great numbers of women who suffered from hysteria were indeed the victims of childhood sexual abuse, then the upper classes who had delivered their hysteric daughters into Freud's

care were rife with sexual predators and perverts. This
was not an acceptable conclusion. Confronted with the
choice between his patients' truth and his social reputation, Freud chose his reputation. In what appears to
be the total absence of any clinical proof, he wrote that
the accounts of abuse he had heard "were only fantasies
which my patients had made up." Upon the wreckage
of his greatest work, Freud proceeded to construct his
theories of psychoanalysis.

The truth of such trauma's commonness demands
social change, and a society resistant to such change will
always deny, discredit, and punish the victims (or advo-
cates of victims) who speak out. It took seven more decades for nascent women's movements to gain enough
strength to induce the change demanded by Freud's original findings, beginning with the feminist consciousness-
raising groups of the 1970s. Their cure was also one of
talking, but this time the listeners were other women,
those with a vested interest in social justice. The services
that we now take for granted, such as battered women's
shelters and rape crisis centers, are the result of those ini-
tial groups and the stories they shared in kitchens and
living rooms across the country.

A similar social change was brought about during

that same time, as veterans of the Vietnam War who experienced symptoms sometimes identical to those of sexually traumatized women also gathered in groups to tell each other their stories. Unsurprisingly, outreach centers and resources were more swiftly granted to these men, along with funded psychological studies whose results were recognized by the American Psychiatric Association in 1980, when post-traumatic stress disorder was included in its manual as an official mental disorder.

Those who benefit from the inequities of our society resist the stories of people whose suffering is in large part owed to the structures of our society. They do not want to have to change. We see this in a thousand forms of white fragility, male fragility, and transphobic and homophobic tantrums protesting the ground gained by trans and queer storytellers. The resistance to memoirs about trauma is in many respects a reiteration of the classic role of perpetrator: to deny, discredit, and dismiss victims in order to avoid being implicated or losing power. Anyone who writes the story of their individual trauma, and especially those of identities that have been historically oppressed and abused, is subject to the retraumatization by ongoing perpetrators: the patriarchal, white supremacist, colonizing nation(s) in which they must live and learn to heal. As Elissa Washuta, a Native essayist, writes: "I am subject to the wants of a country conjured up by invaders who raped, maimed, and killed until they could settle their dream like a film over the land that held the treasure they wanted. Every day, the universe reminds me that, yes, I am safe now, but I am in America. I could be gouged out again."

Social justice has always depended upon the testimonies of the oppressed. We cannot fully acknowledge the harms of patriarchy without a subsequent women's liberation movement, just as we cannot fully acknowledge the harms and continued existence of white supremacist structures in our society without an anti-racist civil rights movement. We cannot fully acknowledge the harms committed against LGBTQI people without a queer liberation movement. We cannot fully acknowledge the violences perpetrated against trans women of color without a movement that affirms the humanity of and demands civil rights for these women. It is not enough for the people of such identities to cast off shame and demand justice. The listeners must join them, and for that, we need to hear their stories.

I'll say it again, because it bears repeating: the resistance to memoirs about trauma is always in part—and often nothing but—a resistance to movements for social justice.

I am lucky that my faith in my creative instincts— facilitated by the many forms of support and privilege that I'd enjoyed my whole life—was behind my own self-doubt and shame, and ultimately stronger than the internalized voices that warned me off writing memoir. It quickly became apparent to me that embodied writing is not in opposition to political writing. In fact, it is the kind of political writing that I am most interested in reading.

Now, I don't doubt that I could write something relevant and dynamic and political and beautiful and intellectual about my own navel. And I don't think it's a stretch to wonder if the navel, as the locus of all this disdain, has something to do with its connection to birth, and body, and the female.[1]

Don't be mistaken: acknowledging all this is important, but it will not get your book published. Being healed by writing does not excuse you from the extravagantly hard work of making good art, which is to say art that succeeds by its own terms. There are plenty of mediocre memoirs out there, just as there are plenty of mediocre novels. I have not noticed the memoir genre cornering the market when it comes to failed books.

I labored endlessly to craft my memoir. But after it was published, I still fielded insinuations that I had gotten away with publishing my diary. Interviewers asked only about my experiences and never about my craft. At readings, I would be billed on posters as MELISSA FEBOS, FORMER DOMINATRIX alongside my co-reader, [INSERT MALE WRITER NAME], POET. Acquaintances, and even some friends, after reading the book, would exclaim to me, "The writing! It was so *good*," as if that were a happy accident accompanying my diarist's transcription.

Writing about your personal experiences is not easier than other kinds of writing. In order to write that book, I had to invest the time and energy to conduct research and craft plot, scenes, description, dialogue, pacing—all the writer's jobs. I also had to destroy my own self-image and face some unpalatable truths about my own accountability. It was the hardest thing I'd ever done. It made me a better person and it made my book a better book.

I prefer to read books that evidence this kind of emotional confrontation with the self. I have the capacity to appreciate masterpieces of craft, but without a certain emotional depth I lose interest. I want more than mechanics, more than experimentation. I want to feel on the page how the writer changed. How the act of writing changed them.

Navel-gazing is not for the faint of heart. The risk of honest self-appraisal requires bravery. To place our flawed selves in the context of this magnificent, broken world is the opposite of narcissism, which is building a self-image that pleases you.

For many years, I kept a quote from Rilke's *Letters to a Young Poet* tacked over my desk: "The work of the eyes is done. Go now and do the heart-work on the images imprisoned within you."

Listen to me: It is not gauche to write about trauma. It is subversive. The stigma of victimhood is a timeworn tool of oppressive powers to gaslight the people they subjugate into believing that by naming their disempowerment they are being dramatic, whining, attention-grabbing, or else beating a dead horse. By convincing us to police our own and one another's stories, they have enlisted us in the project of our own continued disempowerment.

Believe me, I wish this horse was dead. Take a few of many, many such statistics in a grossly underreported set of crimes: the National Intimate Partner and Sexual Violence Survey recently found that 13.1 percent of lesbians, 46.1 percent of bisexual women, and 17.4 percent of heterosexual women have been raped, physically assaulted, or stalked. According to RAINN (Rape, Abuse & Incest National Network), an American is sexually assaulted every sixty-eight seconds, and one in six women the victim of rape or attempted rape. TGQN (transgender, genderqueer, nonconforming) students are more often sexually assaulted than non-TGQN students. Indigenous Americans are twice as likely to experience a sexual assault as an American of any other race. Just as the justice system was not designed to protect or enact justice for all (and often was designed to protect those with the most power from their harms against those with less), the values of literary publishing were not designed to support or promote all stories. This has been shifting in recent years, but I have learned not to overestimate the speed of institutional change. A little bit after a long time of nothing can be easy to mistake for more than it is.

Still, the dominant culture tells us that we shouldn't write about our wounds and their healing because people are fatigued by stories about trauma?

No. We have been discouraged from writing about it because it makes people uncomfortable. Because a patriarchal society wants its victims to be silent. Because shame is an effective method of silencing.

I used to scoff at memoirs and I was embarrassed to admit that I had started writing one. It was a *serious* book, I insisted regularly, not only concerned with my experience but with *ideas*. Now, this practice strikes me as similar to how, as a lifelong feminist who prefers sex and partnerships with women, I have been insisting for my entire life that I'm not an angry man-hating lesbian. That I hate the systems, not the people. Of course I do not hate every man. The very fact that I, and so many women, are compelled to incessantly reassure them of this is more evidence of our continued oppression.

I am still not free of it. To live by my own values rather than the ones prescribed me by a culture that remains invested in my silence is a choice I must make every day.

My second book is about having a sea captain

father, about loving women, about being annihilated and invented by love and sex. Writing it was an exercise in applying my intellect, and the intellects of other thinkers—philosophers, psychologists, holy people, poets—to the raw matter of my own abandonments. It is a book about having abandonment issues.

This sort of admission might make you cringe; before I finished it, I was scared to admit aloud that my book was about abandonment. But white straight male writers are writing about the same things—they are just overlaying them with a plot about baseball, or calling it fiction. Men write about their daddy issues incessantly and I don't see anyone accusing them of navel-gazing. I am happy to read those books; there are masterpieces among them. I just wish that male authors—along with the greater reading populace—were not discouraged from reading such books by women. That women and people of all marginalized identities were not discouraged from writing them. These stories are thought of as niche, identity related, while white and male stories are more likely to be seen as universal, which is an old chestnut of white supremacist patriarchy.

My third book takes the subject of my own adolescent girlhood and uses it as a touchstone to examine the insidious ways that patriarchy conditions us to discipline our own bodies, thoughts, and interactions, even as we actively work to expel those conditions. I did not intend to write a book about girlhood. I did not even intend to write another book that hinged on personal narrative. I simply followed the subjects that came knocking, and tried to answer my own questions about them.

Sometimes, while writing this book, a question intruded: who cares? I snapped out of the reverie of my work, struck by a sudden fear that I was wasting my time, indulging subjects that had already been written about. While the question of *who cares* is an important one for every writer to ask themselves, embedded in my contemplation of it were more than thirty years of conditioning to believe that the subject of girlhood was not worth a few hours of a reader's time. It was a very meta experience, an example of the efficiency of social conditioning. After a lifetime of my rejecting it, it still inhibited my writing about that very process of rejection. *Don't look over here!* it shouts. *No one wants to read about that.*

But you know what? Tons of people want to read about the comprehensive mindfuck of adolescent girlhood under patriarchy. I can't get enough of it, myself. Whenever this insecurity struck, I would ask myself whom, exactly, I was imagining when I imagined that bored or uncaring reader. It was not me, nor any of the people in my life. It was that one guy in my MFA workshop. It was the editor on that conference panel. It was not anyone whose opinion I actually valued. It was not my intended audience. It was the people whose approval I'd been trained long ago to seek, whose stories I'd learned to value over my own.

I kept writing the book, of course. The process continually revealed new layers of conditioning, functions of my own mind that prioritized the feelings and desires of others—sometimes total strangers—over my own. It is through that very writing that I was able to further undo it.

For a long time, I had a very high tolerance for reading books by men, and in which most of the characters were men. Many of my favorite movies were written and directed by men, and starred mostly men. Sometimes I felt embarrassed when I consumed media that featured mostly women, because media like this is often labeled in derogatory ways and dismissed as unserious. Where is the category of dude lit to parallel chick lit? It doesn't exist, like the male-gendered synonym for *slut* doesn't exist, because we are all meant to read and worship those masculine forms. White masculinity is for everyone, while media that features anyone of any other kind of identity cannot be expected to have an audience beyond those who share that identity.

Now that I have rooted that belief out of myself, my tolerance for it is at an all-time low and sinking. Former favorite movies are intolerable. Bring me your books about girlhood, about queer families and sex workers, your trans bildungsromans. I will read them all.

I don't mean to argue that writing personally is for everyone. What I'm saying is: don't avoid yourself. The story that comes calling might be your own and it might not go away if you don't open the door. I don't believe in writer's block. I only believe in fear. And you can be afraid and still write something. No one has to read it, though when you're done, you might want them to. One of the epigraphs of my second book—though it could be an epigraph for my life—is a quote from the British psychoanalyst D. W. Winnicott: "It is joy to be hidden and disaster not to be found."

Almost everything I've ever written started with a secret, with the fear that my subject was unspeakable.

Without exception, writing about these subjects has not only freed me from that fear, but from the subjects themselves, and from the bondage of believing I might be alone in them. What I have also observed is that avoiding a secret subject can be its own kind of bondage.

To William H. Gass's argument, "To have written an autobiography is already to have made yourself a monster," I say that refusing to write your story can make you into a monster. Or perhaps more accurately, we are already monsters. And to deny the monstrous is to deny its beauty, its meaning, its necessary devastation.

Transforming my secrets into art has transformed me. I believe that stories like these have the power to transform the world. That is the point of literature, or at least that's what I tell my students. We are writing the history that we could not find in any other book. We are telling the stories that no one else can tell, and we are giving this proof of our survival to each other.

What I mean is, tell me about your navel. Tell me about your rape. Tell me about your mad love affair, how you forgot and then remembered yourself. Tell me about your hands, the things they have done and held and hit and let go. Tell me about your drunk father and your friend who died.

Don't tell me that the experiences of a vast majority of our planet's human population are marginal, are not relevant, are not political. Don't tell me that you think there's not enough room for another story about sexual abuse, motherhood, or racism. The only way to make room is to drag all our stories into that room. That's how it gets bigger.

You write it, and I will read it.

2

Mind Fuck

Writing Better Sex

Recently, I began a weekend creative writing work-shop with this exercise: *write your sexual life story in five sentences.* Short of gratuitous usage of semicolons, there was no wrong way to do this; the five-sentence story could be as abstract or as concrete as my students wanted. It could be a chronological list of the five most high-topography sexual events in their lives, or it could be a list of images more akin to a surrealist poem. After the allotted five minutes, they all set their pens down with a touch of weary accomplishment. Then I asked them to do it again.

This request was met with stares, some uncomprehending, some with a touch of contempt. I pressed on. The only requirement was that they not reiterate any of the previous five sentences—they could zoom in to a single event, zoom out to a philosophical summary, make it silly, make it emotionally opposite, make it more honest, make it less or more abstract. After they'd finished, I asked them to do it for a third time. A fourth. At this point, many of their stares implied that I was unhinged, sadistic, or simply ridiculous. Eventually they stopped staring and started writing faster. Here's the point: Their writing got better. It became truer. It became more theirs. I told them, *We could do this all day.* I meant: *and not run out of ways to tell that story.* More importantly, they would bear witness to something greater than mere improvement.

Over the years, I've come to look forward to the point in my own writing at which continuing seems both incomprehensible and loathsome. That resistance, rather than marking the dead end of the day's words, marks the beginning of the truly interesting part. That resistance is a kind of imaginative prophylactic, a barrier between me and a new idea. It is the end of the ideas that I already had when I came to the page—the exhaustion of narrative threads that were previously sewn into me by sources of varying nefariousness or innocuity. It is on the other side of that threshold that the truly creative awaits me, where I might make something that did not already exist. I just have to punch through that false wall.

Left to my thoughts—which are driven by pragmatism, ambition, anxiety, and past reference—my conception of creative possibility, of what might comprise my art, is a steadily narrowing doorway. My favorite classes—like my favorite lectures, like my favorite texts—are usually those that remind me of all the possibilities, of the incredible capaciousness of art and my own imagination. There are so many ways to write a thing, so many ways that only I could possibly write it. Over time, we start to narrow our thinking about what a piece of writing—what a certain story—can be, how it needs to be told. Partly, this is because we get attached to the most familiar narrative. We get attached to the one we tell ourselves, because it makes persisting easier. It makes us feel better about ourselves. It excuses us. It excuses others.

The cause of this limiting of our range, of our scope, is inertial: it is the narrative we have been told about ourselves or our stories, and so that's the narrative we tend to tell. I've spent my whole life being prescribed narratives about my own body: how it should and shouldn't look, what it should or shouldn't do, and what its value is. Particularly, I have learned a lot from my culture, media, government, men on the streets of whatever city I've lived in, men whom I have loved and not loved, women whom I have loved and not loved, and even readers and fellow writers—and what I have learned is how my body is mostly good for sex and that sex should mostly be good for men.

The degree to which this education has affected my life is impossible to overstate. It has defined my relationship to my body; all my sexual and romantic relationships; my relationship to food, clothing, money, and, of course, sex. This internalized narrative about my body and its value has governed much of how I think of myself, and what I have spent the minutes of my life contemplating and doing. The great work of my life has been the project of its undoing, of discerning what is possible to undo, what must be lived with, and how to situate what must be lived with, in the mind and in life, so that it does not do the work intended by its embedding: to undermine any power I might have that does not serve men.

My first book, *Whip Smart*, the memoir that I wrote after giving up my Very Important Novel, was, and I guess still is, a deeply unsexy book about sex and sex work. It's also a feminist book about power and money and gender, and how, for a time in my early twenties, middle-aged, mostly married rich white men paid me to spit and urinate and slap and beat on them in sexy outfits. That job, and the book I wrote about it, were ultimately a piece of that work to undo my own mind's patriarchal programming. When I became a domme, I was a lifelong feminist and a hopeless femme. I wanted to wear stockings and stilettos, and I also wanted to be free. I had a deep drive to be wanted by men and a deep shame about that, which of course came from the same source—a brilliant double bind that I thought was expressly my own. I thought that I simply could not reconcile my politics with these desires.

The job seemed like a solution: I could get paid to be wanted. I could dress like a cartoon sex object while kicking men in the balls. I could call the whole thing a feminist endeavor, and maybe it would be true. As a solution, this worked and it didn't. True, I left that job with a far more generous definition of feminism, one that allowed for stilettos and stockings, but it was not kicking men in the balls that earned me the privilege. It was writing the book, which taught me that it was never up to anyone else to tell me how feminist my shoes were. The work of being a domme, although it was often funny, tender, revelatory, and interesting, consisted of enacting the fantasies of men. In essence, it didn't matter if I was kicking men in balls or jerking them off. By the time I quit, getting paid to dress like a high femme and perform erotic acts felt a lot more degrading than doing so on my own time, for my own pleasure. This is certainly not true for all pro-dommes, but it was for me, a young woman who had arrived at the dungeon with the goal of using it to manipulate herself.

While finding loopholes and manipulating my own narrative has helped me survive a lot, those devices never helped me transcend the limits of the value systems in which I lived. I could never have found room for all of me in a definition of feminism that prescribed what shoes I should wear, nor found empowerment in a job defined by my servitude. In both cases, I had to abandon those constraints: the job that might function as a loophole, and the conception of feminism that required it. While false consciousness doesn't preclude true consciousness, it doesn't strike me as a route to it, either. Not in life, and not in writing.

Shortly after that book was published, during a post-reading Q and A, a woman stood up and asked me, "Aren't you ashamed?" It was a rhetorical question, but still I answered it. "No," I said. "I am shameless." This was both true and untrue. I was not ashamed of having been a sex worker or of having written about it, though shame is one of the forces that propelled me into that job.

Later, I wished I had answered with the words of the late great essayist Nancy Mairs:

> Shamelessness, like shame, is not a masculine condition. That is, there is no *shameless man* as there is a *shameless woman* or, as my grandmother used to say, a *shameless hussy*. A man without shame is in general assumed to simply

have done nothing he need feel guilty
about. A woman without shame is a
strumpet, a trollop, a whore, a witch.
The connotations have been, imme-
morially, sexual . . . My sexuality has
been the single most powerful disruptive force mankind has ever perceived,
and its repression has been the work of
centuries.[2]

That is, even after rejecting decades of encouragement
to be ashamed, and writing a book about rejecting that
shame, I was shamed. (I mean, of course I was.) Shaming
is done from the outside and it never ceases.

Those external reactions, many of which I've internalized, have very little to do with my actual body and my
actual sex. They are what I have had to navigate around
or through or what I have to annihilate if I ever want to
write about my actual body and my actual sex.

Writing is, like gender or dominatricing, a kind of performance. But the craft of writing is primarily an art of
making decisions. I often like to terrorize my students

by insisting that every single notation—every piece of punctuation, every word, every paragraph break—in a piece of writing is a decision. You know when something is done, I tell them (they always want to know how to know when something is done), when you know the argument for every single choice, when not a single apostrophe has slipped by uninterrogated, when every word has been swapped for its synonym and then recovered. I don't mean to take the fun out of creation, or even to impose my own laborious process on them, but I actually believe this. Not in the first draft, or even the fifth, but by the end, I want to have stripped as many tics and defaults, as many blind choices as is in my power. I want to be awake to all my choices.

A big part of making creative decisions is relying upon what I guess we can call instinct—the intelligence of the imagination, the spirit, maybe, what we used to call the muse. A big part of instinct is just the cultivated habits that we refer to as skill. However much talent I had as a graduate student, the intelligence of my imagination could not communicate itself very clearly until I had spent some years practicing how not to indulge my strengths and weaknesses alike. This instinct may not be acted upon with great momentary consciousness, but the years of consciousness that cultivated it stand in for that.

What I am interested in ferreting out are those other instincts, the ones we have inherited or practiced for reasons other than our good writing, the communication of our imaginative intellect. Which brings me back to sex: so much of writing that describes it is still performing unconsciously, still comprises a series of decisions that were not so much made by the writer but by the matrix of inherited values that inform the reader's own beliefs around the acts.

Driving out this automatic tendency is easier said than accomplished. When I first starting writing *Whip Smart,* I received two devastating notes, which were essentially the same.

The first was from my graduate workshop, in 2006, the first people to ever read the beginnings of that book. I submitted a twenty-page chapter that detailed a session with one of my regulars. There was spanking, a golden shower, and lastly, some private post-session shooting up in the bathroom. After exclaiming their interest in the subject and praising my sentences—the reactions I had hoped for and been thusly satisfied by—one of my class-mates asked me, "But what were you . . . *feeling* during all of that?"

"I was on heroin," I reminded them, defensively, auto-matically. "I wasn't *feeling* anything."

That wasn't good enough. Because what they already knew, likely more from being lifelong readers than MFA students, was that one of the requirements of memoir, and perhaps of all satisfying or authoritative writing, is that the writer know more about their characters than the reader does. Simply transmitting my impressions of an experience at the site of their happening was not enough. My early drafts suffered from the worst sort of dramatic irony: the unintentional kind. Not only did my readers know things about other people that my protago-nist didn't—that in fact *not* every waitress in Manhattan would have been a pro-domme if they'd known it was an option—but also things about herself that she hadn't en-tirely realized. For instance, that some of the experiences I described were the type to leave an impression, even on a mind smoothed by heroin.

This note led me to take a six-month hiatus from writing the book to conduct more research, primarily in the form of psychotherapy.

The second note came from my psychotherapist. I was so excited to show her my writing, thinking erroneously that she, having come to know me primarily vis-à-vis my persistent anxieties and compulsions, would be amazed by my talents, of which she had previously had no inkling. At twenty-six, I did not yet know that people who are not artists, but have relationships with artists that are not based on the artist's art, care very little about that art. Or, to be more generous, they care about it only insofar as it is relevant to the relationship. After reading a chapter of my memoir-in-progress, my therapist did not comment on its literary merit at all. Instead, she told me: *"You're still acting like Justine."* The truth and incisiveness of this left me thunderstruck: I had allowed the persona I'd constructed as a domme (and named Justine) to author my memoir. I had been telling the story I had been telling myself as those events happened, not the story of what happened.

In a way, I was enacting the kind of literary pornography that Susan Sontag describes in her essay "The Pornographic Imagination," which makes a wonderful case for literary pornography by way of mostly French writers including Marquis de Sade, Georges Bataille, and Pauline Réage. "Pornography," Sontag asserts, "is mainly populated by creatures like Sade's Justine, endowed with neither will nor intelligence nor even, apparently, memory. Justine lives in a perpetual state of astonishment, never learning anything from the strikingly repetitious violations of her innocence." While my persona—unlike his Justine—was carefully endowed with intelligence and will, she was also somewhat barren of insight, motive, or the sort of progressive self-knowledge that we hope for in the narrator of a memoir.

In the larger narrative of my life, I was a fairly well-developed character. I learned and grew and progressed in a somewhat linear manner, though my relationship to sex and desire as represented in my work—and to a lesser extent, my thoughts—was strangely repetitious. Sontag claims that "pornography is a theater of types, never of individuals," and in that sense, the dungeon was a pornographic theater—in its sessions, if not its dressing room, the latter being where we got to know one another's real names and the personalities beyond our domme personas.

In some ways, I had also made a pornographic theater of my own bedroom by so often playing a role in my own sex—especially with men—that was often more informed by cultural indoctrination than my own desires. But no one is a type inside themselves, and no performance is bereft of the actor's own private consciousness. However deeply suppressed, the true story of our experience always plays out simultaneously, and is recorded in the private archives of memory. Unless the writer of these sexual experiences aspires to pornography, this truer story is usually the one more worth telling.

I can succinctly describe this project of differentiation only on the other side of having written a book that depended upon it and with nearly twenty years of hindsight. When I worked as a pro-domme, my own motives were not yet clear to me, nor were the distinctions between my own desires and those coming from outside me, or my internalization of them, or the story I had cursorily written to paper over those realities. In this case, the flimsy story was that I had simply recognized a lucrative opportunity. That commercial BDSM was an inherently feminist enterprise. That being on drugs prevented anything from making an impression on me. That I didn't feel anything but bored, empowered, and high. None of this was true. The work of being a pro-domme was (for most of my tenure in it) not all that well paying, often humiliating, and I frequently felt aroused, ashamed, confused, scared, exhilarated, and bored even while high on drugs, not to mention the oubliette of my truer feelings to which I did not yet have access. This kind of psychological, imaginative, and ultimately aesthetic slumber can be entertaining, particularly if your own thoughts about sex are uninterrogated, but the more my own consciousness wakes, the more banal I find it.

My mother has been a practicing clinical psychotherapist for almost thirty years. Once, I asked her if she ever gets sleepy during sessions. "Rarely," she said, and explained that, for the most part, she finds listening to her patients inexhaustibly compelling. Over the years, she has come to understand that the only time she gets drowsy is when her patient isn't telling the whole truth, mostly to themselves, or when they are not fully awake in their telling. If they are performing a persona or telling her the story they have told themselves and not reaching for the greater truth of an experience, she begins pinching herself. I related, not as a listener of people's stories but as a reader of them.

There are many beautiful and acclaimed books that I have begun and found astute in any number of ways. However, if such a book strikes me as asleep to its own biases, if it lacks that glint of authorial awareness amid the characters' self-delusions, my attention drifts. I wish there were a more technical way to describe this recognition, but it is largely the function of experience. I have written work that is dishonest in this way and, in literature as in life, we who have recovered from a thing are often the best detectors of it.

If using art to tell the story that we have been telling ourselves is boring, then using art to tell the story that we've been conditioned to tell ourselves is even more tedious—a redundancy of a redundancy. Historically, the art that reinforces these scripts—including but not limited to those of gender presentation, compulsory heterosexuality, and patriarchal beauty standards—is partly driven by commerce: the more we believe we ought to be something that we are not, the more money we will spend in that mission. Those who benefit from a dominant power structure want art that represents them, that reinforces the status quo, as they want sex that reinforces the status quo, and the best way to do that is to reiterate it, in literature as in life. The genius of social conditioning is that it is viral and can adapt to any situation a human might enter.

All of this is one explanation why the pornography I watch, the sex I enjoy, and the sex scenes I'm interested in reading are such discrete categories. Which is not to say that a good literary sex scene oughtn't describe sex that plays to social scripts, only that it ought to know that it is doing so—and ideally, why. Having cultivated this awareness in myself—the ability to recognize a sex scene that triggers a conditioned erotic response (like the ones I watch in pornography[3]) and is basically an enactment of ideas I've been socialized to believe since childhood about women's value as sexual objects, and about submission to men as the apex of sexual pleasure—I tend to slam the laptop closed before I've even finished my porn-driven orgasm. Not because I am ashamed to have been watching porn but because once I'm no longer high on arousal and tapped into my deeply ingrained neural pathways, the artifice and depravity of the porn I like to watch bums me out completely. It is not only tedious but frightening and sad. I'm only interested in

joining the theater of types designed to brainwash and
oppress me as a momentary actor; I don't want to hang
out there as myself.

Recently, a friend with similar pornographic pre-
dilections and I together wondered why we don't get
off on porn that mimics our actual sex experiences.[4]
I suspect it is because that sort of porn would rely
upon the internal mechanics of intimacy, which a
video cannot as effectively produce, whereas porn
that is working off the scripts that are already embedded in us requires nothing else to trigger arousal.
"The emotional flatness of pornography is . . . neither
a failure of artistry nor an index of principled inhu-
manity," Sontag writes. "The arousal of a sexual response in the reader *requires* it. Only in the absence
of directly stated emotions can the reader of pornography find room for his own responses." That
is, I don't need the porn I watch to be believable or
relatable in any personal way to get off. If I watched
porn that attempted to mimic my real experience of
sexual intimacy, my standards would become inestimably higher. The power of scripts is that they are
easily transferable, whereas sexual intimacy is entirely specific and cannot easily be simulated. Porn is

probably the lowest-quality entertainment I can consume, made possible by its reliance on these internal scripts, which don't require (and to some extent foreclose) imaginative nuance. In my opinion, the highest forms of art do the opposite: They disrupt our internal scripts and force our thinking to become creative, like the third or fourth round of writing your sexual life story in five sentences. They upend the familiar story and insist on a truer, more interesting one.

Writing, with its room for the reader's visual imagination, has the potential to arouse her in all these ways. As an adolescent, I used to masturbate to literary works of misogynistic pornography, feminist erotica, and serious literature. I loved trashy mysteries, romances, and horror novels, and I thrilled to Jeanette Winterson, Gloria Naylor, and Rita Mae Brown. I could place or find myself in all of it. At that point, however, I'd had very little experience of sex with other people. When I began to acquire more, that sex was profoundly affected by everything I had read and watched. It took me a long time to discern between the satisfaction of enacting a story I'd internalized and the sexual pleasures more specific to my partners and me. It doesn't mean that I don't ever want to have sex that boils down to telling myself a story about a kind of sex I learned to idealize as an adolescent. It means that I can tell the difference.

Here I have reached a kind of thesis, one that I had hoped, in all honesty, to avoid. That to write an awakened sex scene, one may need to be awake to their own sex. The work of discerning artistically between the narratives that have been downloaded into your brain and the ones of your own design—this is work that can only follow the work of awakening to it in your own life.

It would be convenient in many ways if how we live did not so fundamentally inform what we write, but of course it does. From what mysterious place in us does our most inspired work emerge? I believe from some creative intelligence that resides beneath our intellect, a close neighbor to the place where our worst impulses are born. We've spent a lot of time considering the work of disgraced men and agonizing over the question of whether we can still love their work. To this I say: of course. A better question might be: do you still love their work? I've found that while the work of terrible people can be redeeming in many ways—beautiful and politically potent, funny and moving—in the specific areas of their terribleness it tends to fail. The female characters in works of fiction by a writer who has violated women are often two-dimensional objects of obsession, possession, derision, or worship—all violable statuses. Or perhaps the men are all presented as inclined to violate. In other words, the author's imagination frequently fails to transcend his own personal limitations. Once I recognize this in a work, it is hard to unsee, nor do I wish to unsee it.[5]

Like most students of my generation, I grew up being taught to worship the novels of men whose imaginations failed to transcend their personal limitations in this way. Many of my "favorite" books were by these authors.[6] Although my standards did not begin to rise until graduate school, when the cult of the misogynistic white male protagonist/writer began to loosen its hold on my literary consciousness (and literary consciousness more broadly construed by the publishing industry), even as an undergraduate I became so familiar with the ways that men—those in the books we were assigned and those around the seminar table—wrote about women, particularly around sex, that I came to anticipate them with a familiar dread.

I recently wrote a whole book about how I learned to discern and expunge the patriarchal narratives that were embedded in my consciousness. To the extent that it has been possible, that mission has inestimably improved my sexual life as well as my writing about sex. The most meaningful way to awaken to any truer story of your own life is to surround yourself with people and works of art that are also interested in this project. It has also turned out that, for me, writing itself is a primary means of liberating my own mind. When I went back to *Whip Smart* after my six-month therapeutic hiatus, I did not bring with me a fully formed story about my experience. Therapy couldn't give me that. I simply returned to the page with a honed will and ability to find that story.

A memoir is a diorama of experience, populated only partially with the memories we carry to the desk. Part of the work of writing it is that of completing that diorama with many of the memories and experiences that we *did not* have access to during the events that we describe. In order to write a memoir worth reading, I had to recover all my disgust, arousal, humiliation, and fear during those years as a pro-domme. I had to discover what I had felt even when it had been obscured by heroin. In this way, I was finally able to tell Melissa's story as well as Justine's. I was able to describe my role in the theater of types and the person I was beneath the mask.

When something seems difficult, in writing and in life, we tend to make rules around it. We like to assign the trouble we have to the thing that troubles us. It is not we who struggle with sex scenes, but sex scenes themselves that are a struggle, that need to be governed by rules. It is also easier to control who writes sex scenes when there are copious rules for how to do so. But not everyone is equally inclined to follow rules, or punished with equal ease for a failure to do so.

When it comes to sex scenes, the rules say things like: Don't write them at all, and if you do, don't use these words. Don't write them silly, porny, dramatic, tragic, pathological, grim, or ridiculous.

My whole practical thesis around the craft of writing a sex scene is this: it is exactly the same as any other scene. Our isolation of sex from other kinds of scenes is not indicative of sex's difference, but the difference in our relationship to sex. It is our reluctance to name things, the shame we've been taught, our fraught compulsion to enact a theater of types. It is indicative of the lack of imagination that centuries of patriarchy and white supremacy has wrought on us.

To teach sex scenes is to talk about plot, dialogue, pacing, description, and characterization: all those elements that make a captivating scene. A sex scene should advance a story and occur in a chain of causality that springs from your characters' choices. It should employ sensory detail that concretizes and also speaks symbolically to the deeper content of the story. Or if not, it should service your work of art in whatever ways you want from your scenes. Though I am happy to talk about scene building anytime, that's also not how I want to spend the rest of this chapter.

The harder work of writing sex scenes is undoing your own mind's preconceptions about writing sex. Being given rules about a thing can shape your mind. Think of Foucault in *Discipline and Punish: The Birth of the Prison*, writing about the panopticon—the prison model predicated on surveillance that used the internalized eye of the

state to control its prisoners: "discipline produces subjected and practiced bodies, 'docile' bodies." The examples for this are probably infinite, but take for instance the
way I related to my own body for the majority of my life,
how it was determined by the rules I was given for how it
should look. I spent years monitoring and punishing my
own body for being something it was not supposed to be.
One of the ways that I undid that conditioning was by
habituating myself to other ways of thinking. For years
now, I have ended my daily morning journal entry with
the sentence: *Today, I reject the patriarchy's bad ideas.* It's
a needed reminder that when I start to feel bad about
my body or laughing too loud in a restaurant or start to
wonder if I should shave my armpits, those are not my
ideas. I like my body, laughing loudly in restaurants, and
my soft armpit hair.

Sometimes the best way to unlearn something is
by simply cultivating defiance toward those unchosen
rules. Willful, opposite action can counteract their ha-
bitual governance of your writing and thinking. This is
the logic undergirding the concept of affirmations and a
whole genre of self-help books. I believe it's possible to
retrain the mind to write more creatively and truthfully
and smartly about sex, just as it was possible for me to

train my writing out of the bad habits of mixed meta-
phors, passive voice, superfluous modifiers, and a total
lack of narrative tension. As an added benefit, I believe
that doing so will simultaneously train your mind out
of relying on those internalized narratives and habit-
uate you to *thinking* more creatively and truthfully and
smartly about sex.

So, instead of outlining all the bad examples of sex
scenes, thereby reiterating the rules we have been given
in order to rebut them, or using my own preferences
to produce another set of rules that mandates a writer
go to therapy before she writes a sex scene, I recently
started making a list of unrules, intended to release us
from some of the restrictions that have been imposed
on our writing and which we've learned to enforce on
ourselves.

The only restriction I'll impose on the examples I use
is that they won't fall under the umbrella of what Inga
Muscio (in her wonderful book, *Cunt*) calls rapism.[7] It
might seem obvious that I'm not including any kind of
sexual violence in my very narrow collection of favorite
sex scenes, but it's not obvious at all, because for much
of my life I have been presented with examples of sexual
violence as sex.[8] These categories do not exist in isolation

from each other; there are endless connections between sex, trauma, and violence. But for the purposes of this chapter and this partial list, I will use only examples of consensual sex.

Obviously, this list could be hundreds of times longer, and its contents could be tailored to each writer. Our embedded tics are a subjective collage assembled by our relationships to various cultures, classes, identities, and experiences. My hope is that you expand my list to more closely speak to your particular inhibitions.

You can use any words you want.
In my experience, the most commonly repeated rules about sex scenes relate to diction. (No pun intended.) There are only so many words for some things, we say, and these words have been used up: cock, pussy, the likening of women's nipples to pencil erasers.

We are all ultimately writing about the same four or five things: death, trauma, love, loss, recovery. Mostly death. If sex words have been overused, so have grief words. But you don't see folks so readily nixing the use of *sad* or *tears* or *melancholy* or scenes of staring into the middle distance as you contemplate the terrifying sublimity of your own mortality. Not the way you see folks banning the words *pussy, hump, thrust*, or, most terrifying and supposedly unsexy, *vagina*.

The problem is not that *vagina* is an unsexy word. Or that nipples never do look like pencil erasers.[9] The problem is that we have exiled sex in our minds. We have isolated it from the larger inclusive narrative and we have limited its definition to that which serves the most privileged class of protagonists.

I think that this is a symptom of that other habit of treating whole classes of human beings as though their stories do not have the stakes, narrative depth, and complexity typically assigned to dominant protagonists. It is a craft quandary indeed to write yet another sex scene in which a white male protagonist exercises his archetypal masculinity on a secondary, two-dimensional character functioning as a prop in his hero's journey without any narrative awareness of this exhausted trope.

But to write a sex scene in which that marginalized character is treated with some reverence and depth? To write it from their perspective? Or to write a scene in which a white male character experiences, even in an inchoate way, the deep discomfort that occurs when we act out our erotic story on another body without recognizing its humanity? I'll repeat the unrule: you can use any words you want.

Here is Eileen Myles, from *Inferno*, in case you thought comparing a pussy to soup, or using the word *crotch*, was out of bounds or unsexy:

> But after kissing her mouth a little chapped which seemed familiar then feeling her breasts not so large, but nice round and beautiful, familiar breasts, ones I already knew in some way I tugged down her pants. She said Oh. Like a soft amount of light, a small gust of wind. And luckily she had some sweatpants on or something, a stretchy waist. Easy getting them down and there were her lemony legs. Not big not strong, but smooth soft hair like peaches everything that way. Pink rose warm. I just dived down. It couldn't have been too fast. Time was being so slow and warm. And there it was. A pussy, the singular place on a girl, it's where I'm going. Wiggly thing, like soup, like a bowl.

Another mouth. Like lips between
her legs and the taste of it. Piss and fruit.
I pressed my face against its bone and it
moved. She was letting me. All this was
happening. I smelled the future right
there, a present and a past. All that went
through her, known through the soft
sweet flesh of her lips and clit. It was like
my face felt loved temporarily [. . .] I felt
plunged into a tropical movie in which
light was bathing my head and her pussy,
her cunt, her crotch was a warm smile
and for a moment I lived in her sun.

The revelation here is not that these words can be
used in a sex scene, but that a *pussy*, a *cunt*, a *crotch* can be
transformed by a sex scene. "Language is never innocent,"
Roland Barthes once wrote, and I agree. Here, in the
sense that the words *pussy*, *cunt*, and *crotch* all carry the
connotative luggage of all their previous contexts—
the violence, disgust, and pornographic theater of all
the scenes and mouths I've heard them in and from.
Experience, however, *is* innocent. This narrator's sexual
reality is so powerful a phenomenon that it washes these

words of their previous connotations. Now they mean
not *a wimp* or *a bitch* or *the place on a woman that belongs
to a man*, but something magnificent and weird, pure
and exotic, deeply familiar and erotic—a warm smile, a
cosmic body. Just as sweatpants become perfect attire for
such a scene, *smooth soft hair like peaches*, and the actual
smell of sex a good one. When they enter this revelatory
scene, these degraded words are suddenly imbued with
the same reverence as their speaker. To use them is an
incontrovertible act of (re)creation.

Sex doesn't have to be good.
In the full meaning of *good*. Because a lot of it isn't.
True, a lot of sex is not about love, intimacy, or even
pleasure. Sometimes it's driven more by rage or a wish
for escape. Or, in the case of this excerpt from Cheryl
Strayed's essay "The Love of My Life," grief:

> I did not deny. I did not get angry. I didn't
> bargain, become depressed, or accept. I
> fucked. I sucked. Not my husband, but
> people I hardly knew, and in that I found
> a glimmer of relief. The people I messed

around with did not have names; they had titles: the Prematurely Graying Wilderness Guide, the Technically Still a Virgin Mexican Teenager, the Formerly Gay Organic Farmer, the Quietly Perverse Poet, the Failing but Still Trying Massage Therapist, the Terribly Large Texas Bull Rider, the Recently Unemployed Graduate of Juilliard, the Actually Pretty Famous Drummer Guy. Most of these people were men; some were women. With them, I was not in mourning; I wasn't even me. I was happy and sexy and impetuous and fun . . .

I did what I did with these people, and then I returned home to Mark, weak-kneed and wet, bleary-eyed and elated. *I'm alive*, I thought in that giddy, post-sex daze. *My mother's death has taught me to live each day as if it were my last*, I said to myself, latching onto the nearest cliché, and the one least true. I didn't stop to think: What if it *had* been my last day? Did I wish to be sucking the cock of an Actually Pretty Famous Drummer Guy? I didn't think to ask that because I didn't want to think. When I did think, I thought, *I cannot continue to live without my mother.*

Perhaps when Strayed wrote the first version of this essay, it was more infused with the story she had been telling herself just after her mother died. Instead, it is the story of the story she told herself as it was happening, and the greater story in which that story existed, and which could only be told by a narrator who had a wide enough lens to view it.

When I say that sex doesn't have to be good, I mean that it can be awkward, unsatisfying, offensive, and boring. I also mean in the virtuous, moral, or wholesome sense; it doesn't have to be healthy or emotionally intimate. The representation of our sexual lives ought to include the full spectrum. While it's well-known that straight sex is full of fake female orgasms and that homophobic bigots think that all queer sex is depraved, there are few depictions of realistically bad queer sex. This is in part because there are so many fewer depictions of queer sex overall, but it is also due to the phenomenon of image management that often occurs in representations of marginalized communities.

As a queer woman and a former sex worker, I have experienced blowback for depicting aspects of those sexual experiences that weren't wholesome or fulfilling or healthy. Most of us former and current sex workers know that drudgery and dissociation are indelible parts of that work. And all of us queers know that not all our sex is healthy and satisfying.[10] There were plenty of days in younger years when I faked orgasms with women.

I've found that those of us fucking in the margins are often policed by our own communities to represent our sex in an idealized way. I get the logic. There are so few representations of our sex out there that we who find any kind of spotlight must speak well for the whole community. The idealization and marketing of our marginalized sex experiences as wholesome and perfect is a great argument against the argument for our depravity. But it also erases so much of our humanity. Queerness does not have to be healthy to be human. No one of any race need prove their respectability by the sex that they have or purport to have. We do not have to earn our humanity by being any kind of perfect. Ultimately, I think that representing the full range of our humanity is the best argument against its erasure.

Here is a scene from Raven Leilani's *Luster*:

> Slowly, he eases me down onto his grand,
> slightly left-leaning cock, and for a mo-
> ment I do rethink my atheism, for a mo-
> ment I consider the possibility of God as
> a chaotic, amorphous evil who made au-
> toimmune disease but gave us miraculous
> genitals to cope, and so I fuck him des-
> perately with the force of this epiphany
> and Eric is talkative and filthy but there
> is some derangement about his face, this
> pink contortion that introduces the white
> of his eyes in a way that makes me afraid
> he might say something we cannot recover
> from just yet, so I cover his mouth and say
> shut up, shut the fuck up, which is more
> aggressive than I would normally be at
> this point but it gets the job done and in
> general if you need a pick-me-up I wel-
> come you to make a white man your bitch.

Perhaps even more important than the representation
of our fake orgasms is that of our transcendent ones,

acquired by way of acts that might make certain straight readers squirm. Not because it's important to make them squirm, but so the rest of us know that it's possible to make a white man your bitch or get spat on without shame, as Garth Greenwell shows us in *Cleanness*:

> There were things I could say in his lan-
> guage, because I spoke it poorly, without
> self-consciousness or shame, as if there
> were something in me unreachable in
> my own language, something I could
> reach only with that blunter instrument
> by which I too was made a blunter in-
> strument, and I found myself at last
> at the end of my strange litany saying
> again and again I want to be nothing, I
> want to be nothing. Good, the man said,
> good, speaking with the same tender-
> ness and smiling a little as he cupped
> my face in his palm and bent forward,
> bringing his own face to mine, as if to
> kiss me, I thought, which surprised me
> though I would have welcomed it. Good,
> he said a third time, his hand letting go

of my cheek and taking hold of my hair again, forcing my neck farther back, and then suddenly and with great force he spat into my face.

Reading, we often say, is an exercise in empathy. It is entering into the consciousness of a character and feeling what they feel, assuming their concerns. That is why we *show* instead of *tell*, to create a tableau of experience that the reader can enter. Whether or not Sontag is correct when she writes that "everyone has felt (at least in fantasy) the erotic glamour of physical cruelty and an erotic lure in things that are vile and repulsive," it doesn't stop us from rejecting the idea that these aspects might also be, to some lovers, an expression of tenderness, play, or intimacy in addition to dominance or humiliation. Every sex scene that we write has the potential to expand a reader's entire conception of goodness. The idea of *good* may be deeply associated with Judeo-Christian ethics, but the word *good* comes from the Old English *gōd*, which denoted excellence, fineness, and desirability—entirely subjective qualities—and the Old English *gædrian*, "to gather, to take up together." That is, in the oldest sense of the word, mutually satisfying face-spitting is just as *good* as missionary.

Sex is what you call it.

One afternoon near the end of seventh grade, my mother picked me up at the library, where I had supposedly been studying with my friend Stacy. I dropped my backpack on the floor between my feet and buckled my seat belt, but my mother didn't drive. She kept staring out the windshield and finally said, *You smell like sex, Melissa.* Mortified, I stared out of my side of the windshield. *I've never had sex,* I said, believing it was true. *Sex isn't just intercourse,* she said.

File this under things a bisexual mother can clarify for you. Since my teens, when I started openly dating other women, I have fielded (mostly from men) the rude but "innocent" question of how two women have sex. The implication being that sex includes penetration by a penis, that this act is the culmination of all the lesser acts that precede it. Perhaps the biggest inherited narrative about sex that I've had to undo in myself is that default defining of all sex as related to hetero sex. Back then, no matter how I explained it, the askers of that question frowned. *How sad*, their faces seem to say, *that you've never ever gotten past third base.* How sad, I'd now like to reply, that you've been trapped on a baseball diamond for all your sexual life.

Show us what your sex is, what your characters' sex

is. Maybe you, too, have been defining it in relationship to heterosexual models that have nothing to do with your own desire, or that of your characters. This might be hardest for straight people, who have the greatest number of inherited stories to wade through. Discover it in the writing; I often have. The beauty is that we don't have to agree on this. When I was a dominatrix, I once rubbed balloons all over a man for seventy-five dollars. He would've called it sex. I called it work. It was mutually consensual, and I think we were both correct in our assessment.

If your sex is balloons, if it is blowing raspberries on your lover's belly, if it happens fully clothed or in furry costumes, if it happens in a group or alone—give it the same gravity, the same reverence or irreverence as all the tiresome scenes of heterosexual penetration we all grew up reading. In the world of your writing, no sex is a punchline unless you make it one. There is no marginal erotic unless you sideline it.

Here is one of my favorite poems, "Practicing" by Marie Howe:

I want to write a love poem for the girls I kissed
    in seventh grade,
a song for what we did on the floor in the basement

of somebody's parents' house, a hymn for what
   we didn't say but thought:
That feels good or *I like that*, when we learned how
   to open each other's mouths

how to move our tongues to make somebody
   moan. We called it practicing, and
one was the boy, and we paired off—maybe six or
   eight girls—and turned out

the lights and kissed and kissed until we were
   stoned on kisses, and lifted our
nightgowns or let the straps drop, and, Now you
   be the boy:

concrete floor, sleeping bag or couch, playroom,
   game room, train room, laundry.
Linda's basement was like a boat with booths
   and portholes

instead of windows. Gloria's father had a bar
   downstairs with stools that spun,
plush carpeting. We kissed each other's throats.

We sucked each other's breasts, and we left
    marks, and never spoke of it upstairs
outdoors, in daylight, not once. We did it, and it was

practicing, and slept, sprawled so our legs still
    locked or crossed, a hand still lost
in someone's hair . . . and we grew up and hardly
    mentioned who

the first kiss really was—a girl like us, still sticky
    with moisturizer we'd
shared in the bathroom. I want to write a song

for that thick silence in the dark, and the first
    pure thrill of unreluctant desire,
just before we'd made ourselves stop.

When I think of literary works that incite in me the *feeling* of early eroticism, I think of this poem. It does not evoke the first time I had intercourse, oral sex, or even an orgasm with another person—not any of the events that serve as supposed benchmarks in a sexual history. It evokes my "first pure thrill of unreluctant desire"—the first time I got stoned on physical longing. For me, it was in my basement under a mildewy towel with a fellow teammate from Little League. We called it playing "Date," and she always played the boy. That teammate has never shown up on any mental list I've made of my lovers. But if I revise the definition of sex that I inherited from a church I don't belong to, or the interests of a hypothetical man I won't be fucking, then she was my first.

When we define our sex first by those acts that mean something to us, by the consummation of *our* desire, the center shifts. Similarly, when we do this for our characters, they get to stay at the center of their own stories. The scene in which a character's sex is whatever she calls it maintains the continuity of the world created by the writer; it is not injected with some other narrative, one that privileges the desire of a character whom the writer did not create but who exists inside them nonetheless.

Writing about sex doesn't have to include sex at all.
A lot of my favorite sex writing does not include sex by any definition. It is the writing that situates sex in the mind, the emotions, the history, the body, and the world

of the character. Here, we return to that craft issue: sex writing is effective when it writes sex into the lives of characters, into the personal, political, and historical realities that created that character and their desires.

Take this from Carmen Maria Machado's essay "The Trash Heap Has Spoken":

> Once, I thought I saw a woman who looked like me in an amateur porn video. Her breasts hung low, and her stomach folded where mine did, and I couldn't stop watching her. She bit her lip and sucked her boyfriend's cock and rode him and bent over him and laughed and made the most delicious noises. She was beautiful. He looked at her with such reverence. They were, I think, actually in love.
>
> The guy I was sleeping with came over for dinner. I sat him down and played the video and asked him if she looked like me.
>
> He watched it for a few minutes, his eyes softening perceptively. Then he

gently pried my hands off my laptop and
folded down the screen. "Not really?"
he said. "I mean, a little. But not really."
His expression was inscrutable. He was
a nice, kind person, and I could tell he
was trying to find a nice, kind response.
The problem was he didn't know what I
was looking for.

"It wouldn't be bad if you said she
did," I clarified. "I just want to know
what I look like."

Sex, like any experience, is a lens through which we
learn to see ourselves—sometimes a warped version,
sometimes a truer one. We don't have to be fucking to
look through it. Our access to pleasure is determined, to
some extent, by the story we've been told about what a
body like ours deserves. Is a character still acting out the
story she was taught about her body (for instance that it
was mostly good for sex and that sex should mostly be
good for men), or has she written her way out of it, as I
eventually did? Machado's narrator is in the process of
discarding the stories she was raised on about fat bodies

and what they deserve and replacing them with a self-image that is deserving of desire, that feels entitled to physical pleasure. Inevitably, this will affect her erotic life. A character's relationship to sex often reveals more about them than any act can, and characterizing that relationship well will always render a sex scene more meaningful to a reader.

Finally, I'll return to Nancy Mairs, who has written a number of great essays about her own sexuality as well as how the sexualities of disabled people are perceived by the able, with a passage from her landmark essay "On Not Liking Sex":

> The other day, sitting in a tweed chair with my knees crossed, drinking a cup of coffee and smoking a cigarette, I looked straight at my therapist and said, "I don't like sex." I have known this man for years now. I have told him that I don't like my husband, my children, my parents, my students, my life. I may even have said at some time, "I don't like sex very much." But the difference between

> not liking sex very much and not liking
> sex is vast, vaster even than the Catho-
> lic Church's gulf between salvation and
> damnation, because there is no limbo,
> no purgatory . . . I have, [my therapist]
> says, what our society considers "the
> worst wart." In 1981 in the United States
> of America one cannot fail to like sex.
> It's not normal. It's not nice.

The rest of this essay goes on in a similarly humorous, if somewhat glib, manner. I enjoyed it, though I enjoyed more the revision of it she offered in her 1986 collection, *Plaintext*. In it, she claims that the first essay was "true, insofar as any truth can be translated," but also "an exercise in making careful statements that would ensure that I never said what I really had to say." What she really had to say was much more earnest, vulnerable, and compelling. That "in sex, as in the rest of my life, I am acted upon. I am the object, not the agent." This follows an earlier point in the same essay: "I am no original but simply a locus of language in a space and time that permits one—in politics as in sex—to fuck or get fucked." Ultimately, Mairs acknowledges and explores the indelible connection between her experiences of sex as "an act of war" and of being raped at nineteen—her first intercourse.

I am interested in reading about Mairs's voluntary celibacy, but I am even more interested in reading about the previously obfuscated reasons for it that she wrote her way toward a few years later. It reminded me of writing my first book, how I'd had to punch through that false wall to further awaken inside my own story, how it was through the writing that I did so. Perhaps all the writing I love best began as a shallower version of itself—glib and tidy, a theater of types in which we cast ourselves in the role we wish we had played, or the one we were prescribed—a doorway into the truer and more interesting story.

In one of my favorite essays of all time, "Uses of the Erotic: The Erotic as Power," Audre Lorde defines the erotic as far more than the sexual. It is a connection with the self that makes possible deeper connection with others, and can be attained while doing anything—cooking, writing, fucking, fixing a car, or holding a child. The erotic is a "power which rises from our deepest and nonrational knowledge." Once we have experienced it, she claims, we must hold the rest of our lives to that higher standard. "Our erotic knowledge empowers us, becomes a lens through which we scrutinize all aspects of our existence, forcing us to evaluate those aspects honestly in terms of their relative meaning within our lives."

In my life, this means that I haven't faked an orgasm in many years. I don't have sex when I don't want to. I don't stick with the first version of my own life story, and I don't let my students do so, either. It means that I refuse to let the narratives that once infected my thinking also infect my art. This requires a different kind of rigor—in thinking, living, and creation. Whereas writing was once an exercise in transcription, it has become an exercise in transformation. I urge you to hold your own life and work to this higher standard. As Lorde writes, there is "a grave responsibility, projected from within each of us, not to settle for the convenient, the shoddy, the conventionally expected, nor the merely safe."

In order to write well about sex, we must write our whole selves into it; we must place our characters at the center of their own stories. This is an issue of craft, but it is also about joy—the joy of awakening to the full range of human experience, in all its ecstatic, uncomfortable, freaky, transcendent, holy realness. "Uses of the Erotic" is not an essay about sex or sex writing—but in the end, neither is this. It is an essay about the revolutionary power of undoing the narratives we've been taught about ourselves, and how that project might make us not only better writers and lovers, but more human to ourselves.

3

A Big Shitty Party

Six Parables of Writing About Other People

Dear Miss Bankhead:

I thought I was a friend of yours. That's why there's nothing in my book that was unfriendly to you, unkind or libelous. Because I didn't want to drag you, I tried six times last month to talk to you on the damn phone, and tell you about the book just as a matter of courtesy. That bitch you have who impersonates you kept telling me to call back and when I did, it was the same deal until I gave up. But while I was working out of town, you didn't mind talking to Doubleday and suggesting behind my damned back that I had flipped and/or made up those little mentions of you in my book. Baby, Cliff Allen and Billy

Heywood are still around. My maid who was
with me at the Strand isn't dead either. There
are plenty of others around who remember how
you carried on so you almost got me fired out
of the place. And if you want to get shitty,
we can make it a big shitty party. We can all
get funky together!

I don't know whether you've got one of
those damn lawyers telling you what to do
or not. But I'm writing this to give you a
chance to answer back quick and apologize to
me and to Doubleday. Read my book over again.
I understand they sent you a duplicate manuscript. There's nothing in it to hurt you.
If you think so, let's talk about it like I
wanted to last month. It's going to press
right now so there is no time for monkeying
around. Straighten up and fly right, Banky.
Nobody's trying to drag you.[11]

Billie Holiday

The most common question that I have gotten over
the years at readings, in classrooms, and from
friends is how I deal with the fallout of including living
people in my work. I usually first respond by telling them
that there are no living people in my work, only characters, which are figments animated by imagination plus a
small number of qualities shared by the person on whom

they are based. They are a process and a product of radical reduction. The trouble is that almost no one likes to be reduced, even to their most cherished qualities.

I will stick to my own experiences as a way of demonstrating how every writer might develop and follow their own moral compass around this issue. This chapter is not a source of legal advice, though you should request from your publisher a careful legal read of your work if it implicates others. Nor is this a comprehensive list of my own experiences. I could probably fill a book on the subject, but I have no desire whatsoever to write that book; this chapter was hard enough.[12] I've narrowed my own stories down to the six episodes that have most shaped my own ethical code for implicating others in my stories. I've included a list of works that contain far more comprehensive advice on the subject of writing about other people in the bibliography of this book.

If I could write worthwhile books in such a way that it wouldn't upset anyone, I would. Unfortunately, that kind of writing has mostly proved not worthwhile. I often write about the things I can't speak and one of the most common reasons that I can't speak of them is because it would upset people. So, for better and worse, I have faced the consequences, sometimes with more grace than other times. I would change some of my choices, but not many, if I could.

1. *The Foreign Correspondent*

Soon after I'd begun writing my first book, I briefly dated a man whom I and my roommates—my two closest friends—referred to as "the Foreign Correspondent." This was primarily because he was a journalist who'd spent the previous year reporting abroad, but also because we were a trio of very recently reformed addicts and alcoholics, smart young women with filthy senses of humor who had spectacularly failed to fulfill the potential of our precocious childhoods. The Foreign Correspondent, on the other hand, was hyperintelligent, ambitious, and TV handsome. He was squeaky-clean in a way that we'd all been repelled by until we got sober, about six months previous, and still found kind of suspicious. Despite all his exceptional qualities, he was, as we would often say back then, *a civilian*. In our Bushwick loft filled with guitars, empty cigarette packs, and recovery literature, he seemed truly to be reporting from a foreign territory.[13]

He and I didn't have a lot of romantic chemistry—I

was still allergic to any kind of appropriate or available partner—so we stopped dating pretty soon after we'd started, but stayed pals. When I had a near-final draft of my first book, he asked if he could read it and I promptly emailed him the manuscript. As soon as I pressed send, I remembered with a gasp that I had given him a brief and unflattering cameo in the book's third act. I'd included him on a glib list of folks I'd unsuccessfully dated, with a rude reference to my sexual experience with him. I quickly scrolled through my manuscript, deleted the offending line, and emailed him again with the attached manuscript, claiming I'd mistakenly sent an earlier version and could he please read this one instead.

The Foreign Correspondent is a highly perceptive person and a journalist, thus he was tipped off rather than redirected by my hasty cover-up. Within literal seconds, he had performed a well-guessed word search of the document and found the reference. I was appropriately mortified and only more so when he showed the integrity of responding with an apology for his insensitive sexual performance.

There were two lessons here, one more obvious than the other. The first was this: Before showing the manuscript to anyone, consider whether your reader appears in the book and make adjustments accordingly. It's a good idea to do a specific skim of your book to note everyone you mention in it, however peripheral, and consider how they will feel reading your depiction. Otherwise, you will likely face, at the very least, some unexpected awkward interactions later on.

The second lesson was something I realized as soon as I deleted the unkind mention of TFC. I saw that the paragraph was better off without it. A little further along in the publication process, I gave the book the mandatory read to review, for legal and personal reasons, my representation of every character based on a living person. I took out a lot. Mostly, it was details that didn't feel like mine to share, or those which would upset that living person more than they mattered to my book. One of the things that I observed is that when a detail felt cruel, the prose was almost always better off without it.

Cruelty rarely makes for good writing. It can be pleasurable sometimes, both to write and to read, but it is a cheap pleasure. People often rely on cruelty for humor, but again, the prose and people I find funniest do not deploy their punch lines at the expenses of those who cannot defend themselves. In this way, writing cruelly is almost always a form of bullying. No matter what that person might say to you in private, or even on their public social media page after the offending line is published, you will always have the last word. The published word of a writer will last longer than that of any person who is not a public figure. Of course, there are people who deserve it—mostly bullies themselves, but even in the most seemingly righteous situations, I try to trade up from cruelty to some higher form of truth.

2. *Mom Goggles*

When I finished editing my first book, I sent it to every member of my immediate family.[14] I suggested that they wait until they'd finished reading it before we next spoke. I made no promises to change anything. I divulged in my email that while I had told them all that I'd worked as a professional dominatrix and that I was sober, there were details about both of those experiences in the book that they might find surprising and would almost certainly find distressing.

My mother called me immediately.

"Mom," I said. "You're not supposed to call me until after you've read the book."

"No way," she said. "I'm not going to read it, cringing the whole way through in anticipation of these details. Tell me what they are right now."

I sighed. "I wrote an entire book because I couldn't say these things out loud."

"Too bad."

So, I told her. It was not a conversation I'd wish on anyone—mother or daughter—though I am glad she insisted upon it. There are some details in a grown child's life that no parent is meant to know, especially when that grown child has the kind of early adulthood pastimes that I had. Unfortunately, my writing career has made it impossible to spare my own parents.

The next morning at around 7:00 a.m., I was walking my dog when my phone rang.

"Mom! You're supposed to finish the book before you call me."

"I did," she said. "I stayed up all night reading it. I kept turning the light off, but then I'd turn the light back on and keep reading."

"But you know how it ends."

"I still needed to know that you were going to be all right," she said, shattering my heart into dust. "I'm so proud of you," she added. "It was the hardest thing I've ever read. It's wonderful."

I have been both blessed and cursed with a powerful ability to compartmentalize. That is, I was able to write a whole book about being a professional dominatrix and a heroin addict without seriously considering what my mother would think when she read it. It might be difficult to believe, but the first draft of that book had *many* more sordid details than the published version. On the first go-around, I left nothing out.

The most often-repeated advice that I've heard and given on the subject of writing about others is to write the book first. Write it *before* you consider how your mom might feel when she reads it. Write it *before* you start pruning details that will hurt the people you love, or no longer love but care not to hurt. The logic is this: no matter what you think you know about your book before you finish writing it, there will be surprises. We write to understand things. If we already understood them, most of us would grow too bored to complete the immense task of writing a book about them. So, if you begin leaving things out, skirting around or obscuring them, you may be leaving out vital organs that your book cannot live without. Put it all in. After you finish, and you know what parts are *necessary*, you can put your mom goggles on, read it through to imagine her horror at every lurid detail, and cut the unnecessary ones.

"Oh, and one point of correction," my mother said, just as we were hanging up. "You wrote that you moved out when you were sixteen years old, but actually you were *one month* shy of seventeen. It's sort of misleading." She's absolutely right, and I understand why it matters to her, though I wasn't able to apply her perspective thoroughly enough to catch it before she read the book.

   This, and many other similar instances, have taught me that it is difficult to predict what will upset people. I have had plenty of folks tell me confidently that I could write anything I wanted about them. I have come to understand that what they actually mean is that I have their permission to write anything about them *that they can imagine I might*. People cannot give me permission to write the things about them that they cannot see. Or that they imagine I cannot see. We are all so much more transparent than we think. A lot of the time, other people are too preoccupied thinking about themselves and what we might be thinking about *them* to notice, but it is there for the reading if one cares to look. A writer makes it her business to look. There is no way for us to measure our representation of someone against their own self-conception.

When I sent my parents my second book, I still made no promises, but I did say that I was interested in hearing about their responses and that I would do my best to make them as comfortable as possible with the final version.

"There is only one *really* important thing that I have a problem with," my mother said when we spoke. My heart rate increased. She directed me to a passage in which I described her giving birth to my brother, an event that I was present for at three years old, but of which I have no memory. I had described the photos I've seen of the event, in which child me holds a toy stethoscope to my mother's chest. My face is calmly attentive, a tiny doctor on call with a patient, while my mother's expression is tender but anguished. I had speculated about my sanguine disposition despite her birthing screams.

"No woman giving a home birth *screams*," my mother corrected me. "There is no epidural waiting around the corner, nothing and no one to rescue you from the pain. There might have been some guttural *moaning*, but there were no screams."

"Consider it corrected," I said.

Over my three books and many essays, I have put my mother through a gauntlet of information that no mother wants to know about her daughter. She has handled it all with aplomb. In the early years, when I could still hardly bear to talk about the things I wrote, she spared me much of her own difficulties with my work. I know there have been plenty of awkward moments with her own colleagues, friends, and acquaintances, and she has rarely brought these to me.

On the whole, our relationship is stronger for it all. We have had so many hard and important conversations that I would have been unable to start otherwise. In the end, I'm grateful that my work insists upon a degree of honesty that I am not brave enough to attempt in any other form. I am even more grateful—really, immeasurably so—to have someone so willing to meet me there, whose love casts a net wide enough to catch me in all my confessions and cowardices.

I cannot promise this kind of acceptance to anyone, but I wish it for everyone. The only predictable lesson I've gleaned is that when people are upset by what you've written about them, or even about yourself, they will respond as usual. If they tend to denial, rage, self-pity, withdrawal, or acceptance, then that is what you should expect. The act of writing a book is likely to change only one person: you.

3. A Partial List of People I Did Not Forewarn About Their Likenesses Appearing in My Work
My former dominatrix clients and colleagues. All these people used pseudonyms in the dungeon, which, in my clients' cases, I assumed was enough disguise. I doubly changed all my former colleagues' pseudonyms. Now, over a decade later, I wish that I had also shown the book to my colleagues before it was published. My vilification by some of that community was to some extent unavoidable—most people who write accounts of marginalized experience that don't otherwise get much representation find some degree of vilification in those very communities—but some of it *was* avoidable, and I wish I'd known better at the time. While I'm proud of

my first book, which was the best thing I'd ever written at the time, I can hardly bear to read from it today. It has been a valuable lesson in accepting the best
and worst my past self had to offer. Perhaps the more
worrisome thing would be if my ethical sensibility, not
to mention my understanding of craft, *hadn't* evolved
much since my twenties.

Many of my exes. In most cases, I had no current relationship with them that I was interested in protecting.
One of the unfortunate things about writing memoir is
that sometimes it is only a single unflattering detail about
a person or my relationship with them that ends up being
relevant to the story I'm telling. This is impossible to explain to people, nor would it change anything if I could.
One of my exes with whom this happened simply sent
me a message after the book came out that said: "This is
so fucked up." It was fucked up, and I wouldn't include
that depiction if I had it to do over. My motive for including the detail wasn't cruelty, but it also wasn't all that
important.

My close friends. Early on, I sometimes simply didn't
think of it, because they didn't occupy the same space

in my mind that, for instance, my mother did. Nor were they often central characters. Still, I have learned that it is better to show them, if for no other reason than the fact that it is jarring and vulnerable to see a literary simulacrum of oneself in print at the same time that the rendering enters the public domain. Being invited to experience it in the relative privacy that precedes publication mitigates that vulnerability somewhat. It also leaves time to make changes. As I've demonstrated, it's hard to predict what will rankle folks, and this practice, while it maximizes the number of early readers who might seek a legal conflict that would stop a book's publication altogether, it also minimizes such conflicts, because there is time to change small details that might not matter to me or to the story, but matter a great deal to my friend.

Former teachers, former classmates, childhood friends, childhood bullies, childhood paramours, former literary agents, current and former psychotherapists, and former casual lovers. Unless I had a present relationship with these folks, I said nothing and mostly changed their names and identifying characteristics.

4. *Letting the Writer Win*

Once, in a conversation with a writer friend, she asked me how I found the courage to write so intimately when I knew my work was likely to upset the people in my life. I told her that I *always let the writer win*. I explained to her that in the course of my daily life, I was generally a very good employee, a good teacher, a good friend, a good daughter. But when any of those roles came into conflict with my writing, or I anticipated that they might, I was a writer first. I always let the writer win.

Some years ago, I had an experience that changed this. I won't reiterate it here because I do not want to replicate the harm I caused by writing about this person the first time. I will say that it humbled me more than any other experience I've shared in this chapter, more than most things over the course of my whole life. It not only prompted a revision of my personal credo for writing about other people, but also my entire ethical understanding of that exercise.

It is profoundly unfair that a writer gets to author the public version a story that has as many true variations as persons involved. When I think of narrative truth—the truth that lies beyond the verifiable facts of an event—I picture a prism, with as many facets as there are people affected. When a writer chooses to publish their version, that facet becomes the one visible beyond the scope of the people involved. Each person who was present for the events about which I have written has a different true story of them. Their depiction of me in many of those stories would surely hurt my feelings. Probably, I would object to some of their truths, because they conflict with my own. But it has been my version that has been published, over and over. It is hideously unfair. I'm not here to say it is always *wrong*, because if I felt that way, I wouldn't keep doing it. Lots of things that are unfair are worthwhile. However, I do not want to conflate the value of my work with any moral high ground.

Before this experience, I subscribed to a somewhat shallow, self-interested, and, I now see, heartless perspective on this. A kind of *oh well* attitude that was rationalized by a grandiose story about the moral imperative of an artist's vision. This was not something I'd come to by way of deep consideration. It was an attitude of convenience that now strikes me as particularly egregious for an artist whose primary form is the essay, which could accurately be described as an artifact of the process of deep consideration.

Here is what I now believe: I do not have free rein

to write my story of events that happened to someone else more directly than they did to me. If I want to write about my own experience of such an event, then I ought to talk with that person about it *before I begin writing.* I should only publish an account with which they are comfortable. There are lots of little qualifications to this, but they can be resolved using common sense and one's own particular moral compass.

I am glad that experience finally prompted me into deeper consideration of this issue, but I wish it hadn't been at someone else's expense. There are good essays that there are good reasons not to write. Sometimes, it's important to let the writer lose.

5. A Big Shitty Party

When I finished the first draft of the title essay in my second book, I sent it to a close friend and trusted reader. The primary narrative thread in the essay was that of a torturous two-year relationship. I had written most of it while my lover and I were still together, and then finished it shortly after we'd broken up. My friend had witnessed the fallout of everything firsthand, and had counseled me through the breakup.

After she read the draft, she wrote me a characteristically straightforward response. *This is a very beautifully written story,* she said. *But it is not the story of what happened. It reads,* she said, *like you tried to write a version of it that wouldn't upset her. It doesn't make sense.* My friend went on to explain how confusing the essay would have been to read, had she not been able to fill in from her own memory the parts I'd left out. There was no explanation for why the narrator was always crying, my friend pointed out, or even why she had broken up with her lover.

Reading this feedback, my limbs heavied with dread. I had indeed tried to write a version of our story that wouldn't upset my ex, which is to say, that did not inculpate her. I had also tried to write both versions of our story in a single essay: the version I had told myself while we were together, and the truer version I was increasingly able to see after I'd left her.

I went back to the essay and I added some of the parts I'd left out. Not everything, but enough so that the ending made sense. I have asked myself many times, was I fair?

I felt keenly the parts I left out, some of them the ones I knew she'd probably seen as justification for her own behavior. As I wrote my story, as honestly as I was able,

I could see hers, its shape sewn to the edges of mine like a shadow. I had identified with her for two years—that had been the slow work of our relationship, the painful process of adopting her perspective in place of my own. Also, I *wanted* to be able to tell both stories. That felt more fair. Still, I could feel the violation of that narration. Her version was not my story to tell. However confident my assessment of her motives, they remained unspoken, and so to report on them would have been speculative. There were also details from her life that, had I included them, would have made for a more sympathetic portrait of her. Those, too, were not mine to share.

When my mother read the book, she warned me. "With a person like that," she said, "no perceived hit goes unre-turned." I knew it was true. I decided that I was willing to accept the consequences before I published the book. As a wise friend recently said to me: "I don't expect publica-tion to be free of personal and professional cost."

I told the lawyer employed by my publisher to advise me under the assumption that she would try to sue me. He advised me to change so many details to obscure her

identity that I balked. I told him that I had documenta-
tion of everything that I claimed in the book. It didn't
matter, he said. I had to change so much that it felt like
another layer of betrayal, though it was meant to protect
both of us: her from recognition, me from her. It worked.
Frequently, I encounter people who know her and who
praise the book, who have no idea. I'm glad for this. If I
could have written it in such a way that absolutely no one
knew it was her, I would have.

She would have remained even more anonymous had
she not, as my mother predicted, come for me, but she
did, in some very canny ways, and that experience was its
own special hell.

Though it consumed much of my publication experience, I never responded. I was wracked by terror, and felt
for many months as if I was in a small crowded room in
which my ex was spewing convincing arguments to publicly discredit me. Some of what she said felt so untrue
that it was difficult not to respond. I imagine that this is
also how she felt reading my book, my truths that likely
conflicted with some of her own. But in the end, I did not
want, as Billie Holiday allegedly wrote her ex, Tallulah
Bankhead, "to get shitty" and "make it a big shitty party."

I did not want to "get funky together." I trusted that my ex knew better than I how to get funky and make a big shitty party. All I had was the story of our relationship, my truth of the experience, and that I had already told. I had not weaponized that story, and I had nothing else to sharpen against her, nor a wish to hurt her.

The year that followed my book's publication was physiologically reminiscent of the time I'd spent involved with her. Every time I saw her name, my arms shook, my throat went dry, and I felt a sensation very much like a cold hand laid on the back of my neck. This was often how I had felt when I saw her name on my cell screen when we were together. Back then, I had changed her contact in my phone—to initials, to an emoji—multiple times in an effort to reduce that panicked response.

My anxiety reached such heights that a friend suggested a spell. *A spell?* I said, but who was I to refuse any kind of solution? As per my friend's instructions, I wrote my ex's name on a scrap of paper and submerged it in an empty gelato container that I then filled with water and wedged deep in my freezer, behind the ice cube trays and ancient veggie burgers. As far as I could tell, after that, she stopped trying to ruin me. Probably it was a coincidence. Still, when the refrigerator in that apartment broke, I dug out the pint of frozen water and jogged six blocks to relocate it to a friend's freezer. My friend no longer lives at that location, but her former roommates still do. As far as I know, there it remains, her name suspended in ice.

Despite all of it—the shaking hands, the panic attack I had on a tiny plane in the middle of my book tour, the cool phantom hand that I felt every time I saw her name for three years after I published the book—I never regretted writing that story. She did not ruin me, ruined only a good part of my publication experience. My book did not ruin her, either. She is widely celebrated, and I'm content with her success.

I had often been furious at my lover when we were together, but I was never angry while I wrote about us. When I wrote that truer story of our time together, I was not so riddled with fear as I had been when I'd lived it. Fear, like pain, can narrow perspective to a pinprick. It is necessarily self-centered. I could not hold on to the fuller picture in that state and for a long time I did not want to. Through the writing, I became able see more of her humanity, and the ways we had both worked extravagantly hard in our relationship. We had tried our best and we had both failed miserably. That is not the kind of love I want or have today, but it was a kind of love. Love does not preclude harm. Back then, I thought perhaps it guaranteed it. I'm glad I was wrong about that. By the measure I now understand it, I think I loved her best of all while I was writing our story.

6. Creative Nonfiction

The only person whose likeness appears in my work and to whom I show my early drafts is my wife. She is the first reader of most of my essays, and the sole person who gets absolute veto power about any details related to her or to our relationship. Rarely has she ever exercised that right, though she does tease me about sometimes massaging the chronology of events. "Creative nonfiction!" she shouts with gleeful irony. "I said that to you on a completely different afternoon."

Her generosity in this area strikes me as utterly congruent with her manner of loving. She is not threatened by my version of events. Partly, because she benefits from all the previous lessons I have learned; I am a more conscientious writer than I have ever been. Partly, because as a writer she understands that a difference in individual truths is not always a conflict. So long as we don't try to speak for each other, there is room in our house for more than one story.

4

The Return

The Art of Confession

I.

There is a genre of love ballad that I am a sucker for, and it includes a range of styles—from James Brown's "Please, Please, Please" to Usher's "Confessions." My own beloved does not share my predilection for these plaintive, often abject tunes. As she once said, with not a little disdain, "that's a beggin'-ass song."

Beggin'-ass songs have always been my favorites. Songs whose longing often has a ragged edge, a need to love and be loved, and, more often than not, to be forgiven—for misdeeds, misunderstanding, or fundamental flaws. The singer has strayed from the path that leads to the one they serenade and they now wish to return. The voices that sing these songs tie a ribbon round a similarly tender part of me and pull with recognition.

My favorite Christmas carol as a child was "O Holy Night," and it still is, because hearing the command to *fall on your knees* provokes some deep and abiding longing in me: to fall on my knees, to prostrate myself before something and be found lovable, to *hear the angel voices*, to be struck with wonder, to be let in.

I was raised by a Buddhist and a staunch ex-Catholic. I've often thought that if I had been exposed to any kind of church music as a young person, but most of all gospel, I might have been called toward another path entirely. In many cases, *beggin'-ass song* can be another name for hymn.

"How infinitely passionate a thing religion at its highest flights can be," writes William James in *The Varieties of Religious Experience*. "Like love, like wrath, like hope, ambition, jealousy, like every other instinctive eagerness and impulse, it adds to life an enchantment which is not rationally or logically deducible from anything else."

I did not have religion as a young person, but I did have a revelation in my early twenties, just as I was getting sober and opening to the idea of having a higher power in my life other than heroin. That whole time was rich with epiphanic moments and this one arrived one evening as I sat alone in my one-room studio in Williamsburg, listening to a Stax Records compilation.

As I savored the predictable swoon of feeling that "I Forgot to Be Your Lover" and "The Life I Live" generated, I suddenly understood that the soul music of the sixties and R&B of the nineties were my favorites, not, as I'd thought until then, because I was always falling in love, though I was, but because I had what William James called an "instinctive eagerness." My romantic interest at the time was a questionable character whose appeal was already waning and had anyway never been worth the pleas of Bettye LaVette, Bettye Swann, or Betty Wright. The people whom I conjured in my mind when I listened to such singers were simply convenient proxies for something I hadn't yet decided to believe in. I was less a love addict than a person with the kind of beggin'-ass heart that longed to return, not to the arms of whatever person

I was infatuated with, but to something greater, something people of religion might call god.

When I was a kid, my grandmother would sometimes take me with her to Catholic Mass, something my father would no doubt have objected to, if she'd asked, which I'm sure she didn't. Sermons were deadly boring, but I was mesmerized by the aesthetics and the ritual of Catholicism. Even as a little girl I was the kind of femme who loved baseball and pink satin equally, and all that velvet and gold brocade, candles and goblets and incense made me swoon. I wanted the outfits for my dress-up trunk, to take that wafer in my unbaptized mouth, to wear the miniature wedding dress for my confirmation, but most of all, I was drawn to confession.

I longed to enter that slim, beautiful cell—like a coffin for my secrets—and spill it to whomever was on the other side. I didn't think of the priest, though. I didn't even think of God, for I knew no god. But oh, how I wanted to pray. I imagined entering that narrow door and leaving something in the darkness that would render me changed. I did not feel guilty of anything, per se, but if penance was the price of unburdening, I would pay. I did feel burdened. How I wanted to know myself infinitely lovable, wanted to be bathed in the relief of a divine love. In the years that followed, I sought this in many ways, and some of them ultimately became the very things I wanted to confess.

The word *confession* has been traced back to a Latin root meaning "to acknowledge." The aspects of guilt and repentance were added later. I had plenty to acknowledge. The unspoken parts of experience: the lonely, the existential, the erotic—how was I to know they weren't mine alone? These don't seem now like things to feel guilty of, or to disavow, but I didn't know that as a child. How hard it can be to differentiate the unspoken from the unspeakable. I was a sensitive and secretive child, as many are, and that is a lonely condition.

It might be more useful to think of that other definition of redemption. Instead of a deliverance from sin, a buying back, a return of another kind. If I brought my burdens, my unspoken and perhaps unspeakable thoughts and deeds, maybe I could exchange them for the mercy of acceptance.

You wouldn't be blamed for assuming that when my parents first offered me therapy at ten that I took to it eagerly, but I didn't—that took a few more years. At ten,

I didn't want to talk to a stranger. I had already found my confessional.

I remember sitting at the wood desk in my bedroom, writing poems in a thin green ledger meant, I think, for accounting. I was already an obsessive list maker and loved the orderly geometry of lined paper. An empty notebook was a promise. A stack of empty notebooks? Insurance that whatever amount of language might fit inside of each lean binding, that same amount of what filled me could be organized into straight lines, packed onto a train of sense or story that moved inexorably in a single direction. Whatever chaos existed in the abstract, it could not help but submit to the perfect blue lines of a page. Secretive people are often diarists, I've noticed. Even to write unspoken words multiplies them, makes us less alone.

I used notebooks as diaries from a young age, but also when I wrote stories and poems, clumsy emulations of the books I read. Even the most fabricated of these helped quell the tumult inside me. I read madly, obsessively, an eclectic assortment of literary and young adult fiction, horror and romance novels, psychology books, and poetry. These escapes made my childhood bearable. Not because I had a difficult childhood, but because childhood is difficult: powerlessness assured, trauma un-avoidable, consciousness a weird and indefinable burden that we have no way of contextualizing.

The relief of narrative immersion, the power of exter-nalizing and naming my own experience, the pleasures of language and creation—there was no hierarchy between these; I valued and often experienced them as one. It makes perfect sense to me that they became so central to my self-conception and to my life, even at that young age.

I was praised early in school for my verbal skills. My vo-cabulary was bizarrely ornate for a child as a result of my feverish and far-flung reading habits. I remember being complimented on a poem I'd written in fourth grade, and likely began calling myself a writer around the same time. Sometimes I wonder now what the adults and other chil-dren thought of me, this child who called herself a writer, who, when asked what she was going to do when she grew up, often simply said "live in New York City." Probably, my hubris and precocity were either charming or obnox-ious, depending on the audience. In the far reaches of her basement and attic, my mother still finds creased folders of poems and stories written in my penciled cursive, little books with hand-glued or -stitched bindings and my name on their covers.

The first story I learned about writing was that of the agonized writer. There is a robust narrative of this in American culture at large, though I came to it through the words of writers themselves. At a young age I read the poetry of Sylvia Plath and Sharon Olds, and at least knew of Virginia Woolf.

I remember having a copy of Anne Sexton's collection *Live or Die* when I was twelve or thirteen. When I look at the book now, I marvel at my child-self and her ability to comprehend Sexton's unsettling lyrics. I was not suicidal, but I already knew other kinds of "almost unnameable lust," and felt immediate relief at her articulations of interiority, depression, and desire—the things no one seemed to talk about. "I was tired of being a woman," Sexton admits in that book. My body had only just developed, but like her, already "I was tired of the gender of things."

I loved stories of addiction, sexual mavericks, and madness, like *I Never Promised You a Rose Garden*, *The Bell*

Jar, Tristessa, The Basketball Diaries, A Spy in the House of Love. In daydreams, I imagined myself sometimes as the architect of such stories, sometimes as a character in them. I am surprised that it took as long as it did for me to realize that I could be both.

In books, I found an archetype that could hold my own sadness, the loneliness of consciousness and the implicit knowledge of its furthest extremes, that could even make it romantic.[15] The role of *writer* was the first that suggested a way for me to fit into society, to be valued and legible to others, if I were to be consumed by my least nameable hungers, as I feared. Also, that I was not alone. Poets were the first people I found who named those absurd, ugly, unbearable, and ecstatic parts of being human. They are often better named by lyric means.

It is from poets like Plath and Sexton that we have gotten our most contemporary understanding of the word *confessional*—its maudlin connotation. People have always liked to read confessional work, and they have often liked to denigrate it as well. It was a popular style, then it wasn't, then it was again.

The divulgences of the poets helped me decide that I wanted to be a writer very young because *writer* was the only role I could see myself occupying in society, the only one that might hold everything that I was: queer, overly emotional, burdensomely perceptive, reluctant to do any kind of work whose purpose was opaque to me, ravenous in ways that made me an outlier. It was an occupation that seemed to offer respite and relief, but also was connected to the sublime—it offered the gift of self-forgetting, a transcendence on the other side of which lay insight. I did not think to compare this with any description of religious experience, because I had not read any. Now, it seems obvious.

I experienced the urge to write, in the words of William James, "not as a dull habit, but as an acute fever rather." James was referring to the sincerely religious, not the child diarist, though it was with religious enthusiasm, a kind of fanaticism, that I took to writing.

2.

When I got sober in my early twenties, I spent some time making a study of different religions with an eye to one that might suit me. I went to Quaker meeting and Unitarian Universalist service, attended a Zen center, and read a lot of books I found in the spirituality section of the bookstore. What I found was never persuasive or appealing enough to convert me—I remain someone who identifies as spiritual but not religious, but I did look into the practices of confession and found that, the costume and set design notwithstanding, it was not the Catholic tradition of repentance but the Jewish one that appealed to me most.

The medieval Jewish philosopher Maimonides writes in depth about the process of repentance in the *Mishneh Torah*. *Teshuvah*, the Hebrew word for this process, translates to "returning." He outlines it in three phases: stopping the action and resolving to change, relating to the past, and the act of confessing. When delineating this first step, Maimonides cites Isaiah, which reads (from the King James Bible): "Let the wicked forsake his way, and the unrighteous man his thoughts: and let him return unto the Lord, and He will have mercy upon him; and to our God, for he will abundantly pardon." To stop a wayward behavior, Maimonides claims, one must begin from this internal resolution, a determined will. The philosopher emphasizes the change in the confessor's heart over the mercy of God. The whole set of actions that follows depends upon the forgiveness and acceptance of God, but that acceptance is assumed, if the confessor begins from this change of heart.

My first attempt at nonfiction, after years of writing fiction, became a chapter near the end of my first book. When a professor of mine in graduate school told us to write a short memoir, I wrote about the first memory that came to mind. I did not think then about the irony of the fact that the first transparently autobiographical text I ever wrote was an account of an experience of which I had never spoken to anyone.

About two years into my tenure as a pro-domme, men paid to dominate me. My job had, until then, consisted entirely of me dominating them, which was easier to situate with my politics, however ultimately irrelevant they were. Not so, the times I fell on my knees, crawled, begged, and submitted to lashings both verbal and physical. I did not know why I had done this. My feelings about these experiences were a medley of disgust, satisfaction, pride, shame, and confusion. My motives had been erotic, yes, but not only.

I don't believe in memory as a kind of jukebox that randomly selects cuts from the past to play. Nor do I believe that our memories are all manipulated into fantasies, though they are a pliable material. I suspect that everything we remember has symbolic meaning, is redelivered to us as a suggestion, a lesson, a reminder, or else perhaps a haunting, a ghost consigned to the human realm until it completes some bit of unfinished business. Such was the case with this memory.

We associate the word *regret* with a wish to undo or to not have done, but its origin is in the French word for looking back with longing or distress, at something done or undone. It is less oriented to guilt than to disorder.

My longing to return to the past was a question: *why?* And perhaps also: *who?* I was more ashamed of my unknowing than of my actions. I knew that kink was nothing to be ashamed of, but my self-conception was not that of a submissive, and for me at twenty-five, a lack of self-knowledge *was* a cause for shame. Unsurprisingly, I was obsessed with control in those days, though of course I didn't know it.

When I sat down and described the surprising pleasure of physical humiliation for the first time, I had recently undergone what Maimonides might have called a change of heart. I was still taking a session here and there, reluctant to let go of my favorites, and my best-paying private clients, but I had pivoted in my life and stepped toward a new course. I was sober, and had finally faced the ways that my work as a domme chafed against my shifting values. I wanted to grow beyond the persona I'd inhabited as a domme and an addict—not because of what those identities meant to society at large, but because of what they had meant to me, the ways they'd constrained my perceptions of everything. As soon as I clarified that intention, my story stepped forward, demanding to be told.

There is a conventional wisdom about memoir that claims a writer must have sufficient hindsight in order to write meaningfully about her past. This has not been my experience. All that has been required of me to write about something is this change of heart. A shift toward, or away, or perhaps a desire to return to some truer version of myself. I don't even have to know that I've made it, but when I look back at the beginnings of everything I've ever written, there it is.

I recently reread Natasha Trethewey's exquisite memoir, *Memorial Drive*, in which she explores her mother's murder by an abusive ex-husband in 1985. After the murder, the nineteen-year-old Trethewey willfully chose to walk away from the site of that trauma and did not fully face it, it seems, until writing this book. In it, she reflects on her choice to move back to Atlanta sixteen years after her mother's death, when she and her husband bought a house just a few miles from the site of the murder. At the time, she had no conscious intention to confront the past. Of course, a confrontation with it was inevitable. "All those years I thought that I had been running away from my past I had, in fact, been working my way steadily back to it," she writes. In this articulation, I recognized a familiar shift, a psychic (and physical) movement toward a subject before we know consciously what that deeper part of us has chosen.

This change of heart has manifested for me in many different ways, rarely recognizable at the time that they happen. Often it is signified by an urge to write. This is one of the ways that craft and what I have called instinct elsewhere in this book interact with psychology. Here, I will call it inspiration, a sister to the word *spirit*, both of whose origins trace back to the Bible, meaning to breathe into or animate with an idea, and also the essential nature or character of something. *Inspire*—an apt word for the change of heart that precedes a return. Also, the beginning of art.

Another example: In the spring of 2013, I was in the grip of that torturous, addictive relationship. I had made a person my higher power, and all who have done so know its torment. It was a form of worship that held me in bondage, as all obsessions do. I thought of her all day and night and would have sacrificed almost anything to secure her love, or rather, to stabilize the quaking insecurity of our attachment. I ended up sacrificing quite a lot, by the end of it. Though I had not been much of a crier since childhood, I cried so often that the skin around my eyes had begun to peel in dusty flakes.

One evening, near the end of a long and terrible cry, unsatisfying as all my cries were in those days, their churn in me repetitive as the scrape of rubber against the pothole in which it is stuck, I had a flash of inspiration: *I would write the story of this*, and that story would be called "Abandon Me." I found an index card, scrawled the title on it, and tacked the card to my kitchen wall. No title had ever come to me like this, and none have since. It felt so clear and so certain, I understand why the Greeks assigned such moments to the will of powers beyond the self.

But it was not a gift from any muse. It was an act of resilience, the result of all the ways that art had rescued me in the past. It was an intention, a decision come from deeper than my conscious mind, a wish, a prayer— sometimes these can all be synonyms. It was a shift of heart, as embedded in that urge was the desire to leave her, to free myself, because I could not tell that story correctly without doing so.

There the card stayed without addition for the better part of a year. A year in which I continued crying, and in which I wrote a small handful of essays. These essays were unlike any I had written before. They depended less on narrative than a lyric sense. Sunk deep inside the experience I was attempting to describe, I had no perspective. I did not have access to a narrative except the one my lover and I colluded in, which seems increasingly far-fetched the further away from it I get.

There was relief in the meticulous process of massaging these sentences out of myself. I was writing about my affair and my feelings, but, at least while I was writing, I didn't have to feel them the same way. It has been like that since childhood. An analytical part of me takes over when I write and creates a distance between me and the subject, and in that space I have always been able to breathe. Like a cracked door the cold seeps through, so did the truth begin to seep into me.

I would stare up at that index card multiple times per day. It comforted me, like a superstitious tapping of the newel post each time one descends a staircase. Though I never thought this in words, it reminded me that there was a way out, that there was a way to make my suffering useful. Beautiful, even. I had only a foggy idea of what the book it referred to might consist of. I had no idea that I was already writing it.

What I have described is a creative experience, a moment of *inspiration*, and isn't it also a spiritual one? The decision to transform my suffering into art related to my spirit, certainly—for my essential nature and its expression had changed in that relationship such that the people who had known me longest said in nearly identical ways afterward, "you were *gone*." That index card signified my spirit's rebellion, the assertion of my nature as it had existed before her and would after. It was the shovel with which I would tunnel my way out.

The decision also related to my religious belief—I

worshipped that woman more fervently than many have their deities, and embedded in my decision to write about our relationship was the intention to abandon that worship. My art will tolerate no false god. My older faith was in the power of telling my own story, which had demanded truth so many times before and thus transformed me. It was a gospel with the power to cure.

From Pierre Janet's 1889 delineation of the stages of recovery from hysteria, to groundbreaking studies of veterans with combat trauma, to the consensus of many therapists who work with victims of domestic violence and sexual assault, the progression of trauma recovery often takes a recognizably common shape. It is frequently described as a continuum of healing comprised by three approximate phases: the establishment of safety, constructing or completing the narrative of the trauma, and the return to social life.

The first phase is crucial. All forms of trauma—from intergenerational or historical traumas to those of illness, mental and physical abuse, and the many wrought by war—share the quality of disempowerment. No productive therapeutic work can be done until the traumatized patient understands that she has recouped some sense of her own agency. An integral part of achieving this is acknowledging in some form that the traumatic event(s) occurred. This happens cognitively, through the verbal articulation of the present, and perhaps even more importantly, in the body.

Peter Levine, who first developed somatic experiencing, a body-oriented approach to trauma therapy, describes it as one in which "you initiate your own healing by re-integrating lost or fragmented portions of your essential self. In order to accomplish this task, you need a strong desire to become whole again." That desire to become whole is a necessary starting point from which to establish stable ground for healing work.

An understanding of the safety necessary to confront trauma partially undergirds the advice to write memoir with a substantial temporal distance from the experience. So much of what we memoirists write about qualifies as trauma; it is sound advice. Sometimes the art is first one of patience. If we try to write the story of our trauma before we have established a certain degree of psychological and physical safety, we risk doing ourselves more harm. Think of the rape victim, retraumatized by having to repeat her story in its immediate aftermath to an audience of strangers.

What of the experience that lies in the realm of the traumatic, but is of the more ordinary variety, or is complicated by the fact that its victim is also its perpetrator? Addictions, for instance. We often describe the compulsions that disempower us as though they were autonomous characters—the eating disorder or heroin dependency that whispers persuasively in our ear as our bodies disintegrate. These forces are as much a part of us as the selves we wish to return to, or to become in our recovery.

   I wrote about my addiction to drugs before I stopped doing them, yet I did not have access to a perspective that could yield insight about the experience until I stopped. Something also needed to shift in order for me to write about the relationship at the center of *Abandon Me*, though I didn't need to establish abstinence or safety in the same way. There was an external force in the situation: my lover. But my greatest obstacle was still internal. Therefore, the experience didn't need to end for me to recoup some sense of my own agency. Empowerment often begins more subtly, with only a narrow ledge inside ourselves wide enough to hold a crumb of resistance. The "strong desire to become whole again" can occur from the inside of experience and is itself a realm of safety, however small and strobing. I now understand that moment when I pushed the tack into the wall, pinning my future book's title like a neon sign flashing *here*, as a change of course and a change of heart, a beacon announcing a safe location to confront the truth.

One last example. I had given a glancing treatment to the hardships of my girlhood in almost everything I'd written until the age of thirty-five. They crept into my writing over and over, though I never devoted anything expressly to them: the harassment in middle school when I developed early; my consenting to countless sexual interactions about which I felt ambivalent at best, including an early one with a neighborhood bully who had spat on me repeatedly; and my adolescent rebellion. My familiar understanding of these events was that they were no big deal. Shitty, indeed, but a far cry from *traumatizing*. I thought that my rebellion at twelve had been unwarranted; I had a loving family, after all. It was not lost on me that my behavior tracked over a lifetime mapped disturbingly close to that of someone who *had* been traumatized, but I told myself (and anyone else who ever pointed it out) that those were merely the symptoms of genetic addiction from which I was thankfully in recovery.[16]

It is true that I have the mental, spiritual, and physical disease of addiction, and also that this story I told myself was a rationalization, an exploitation of one pathology to obscure the existence of another. Which is to say, a form of denial. I could not look at those experiences or that time in my life with any true depth until I faced the truth of them, or at least became interested in that project. Until I had that particular "strong desire to become whole again."

My first step toward a retelling of that time was an essay about spitting, how it was my favorite thing to do to my clients as a domme. Can you see where that led? Reflecting on this timeline of relation to my past, I think of D. W. Winnicott's words: "Artists are people driven by the tension between the desire to communicate and the desire to hide." I wrote my way into a memory of that neighborhood bully, how I'd worshipped him and how he'd abused me. *Abuse*, a word I've spent tremendous effort to avoid. Suddenly, there was no getting around it.

Something had shifted, and I was ready to look at all that had happened and what it had actually meant. That essay became the first in my third book, *Girlhood*.

3.

It is important for me to be clear: not every memoir tells the story of a trauma. Just as no serious trauma will be completely healed by writing a memoir on the subject. My juxtaposition of these two processes is an analogical exercise, not one of equation. There is plenty of crossover—trauma in memoir, healing through writing. But they are vastly different undertakings. It might be easy to confuse or conflate these processes, so profound are their symmetries.

The second phase of trauma recovery, and the primary work of it, is to tell the story of the trauma. Judith Herman writes: "This work of reconstruction actually transforms the traumatic memory, so that it can be integrated into the survivor's life story." As anyone who has recovered from trauma knows, this is slow and ambitious work. Hurrying it will only incur symptoms that, in addition to the risk of retraumatizing the survivor, inhibit the work of reconstructing the trauma narrative. "Moving slowly and allowing the experience to unfold at each step allows us to digest the unassimilated aspects of the traumatic experience at a rate we are able to tolerate," explains Peter Levine.

Like the trauma survivor, the memoirist cannot hurry her process without impeding it. She must be awake in the telling. A detached reiteration of a detached experience can provide neither insight nor healing. A century ago, Breuer and Freud wrote in *Studies on Hysteria* that "recollection without affect almost invariably produces no result." This is true of both literary and therapeutic storytelling. I have read memoirs that unfold with the texture of unprocessed traumatic memory. The prose in such a book may be technically astute, but it is also repetitive and opaque. As Herman observes, often "it does not develop or progress in time, and it does not reveal the storyteller's feelings or interpretation of events." There is literary work that *intends* to represent this state of mind, which is distinct from work that involuntarily reflects the mind of its author, and can access only this fragmented impression of the traumatic experience.

I have often, and elsewhere in this book, described writing as a diorama that I populate not only with my accessible memories, but also the memories that I must recover in order to tell the complete story, memories of details, emotions, and sensations that I did not have access to during the events, because my priority was to survive them with a minimum of suffering. Sometimes I was on drugs, or escaped into a preferable fantasy, but more often than not it was a mechanism that engaged without my awareness.

The clinical term for going numb to certain parts of experience as a tactic of psychic self-preservation is *dissociation*. Not all forms of detachment from experience are dissociative, but they serve the same function: to avoid the discomfort of an experience we feel powerless to interrupt. The detachment that I have experienced from intimate physical acts that I have consented to but which I did not enjoy is not the same as that experienced by someone in a violent highway collision, or a rape victim, or even the deadening experienced by the worker who is submitted to decades of grueling and repetitive labor. But these are analogous. The writers of all these stories must perform a careful and often painful recovery of the memories of those exiled sensations. Just as the trauma survivor must do to the tell the story on which her recovery depends.

For the trauma survivor, this storytelling must also happen corporeally. Trauma is described in many ways as an interrupted experience not only in the mind, but also, and perhaps even more profoundly, in the body and its systems. Healing depends upon what therapists who practice somatic experiencing call biological completion. Resmaa Menakem, in his groundbreaking book on healing racialized trauma, *My Grandmother's Hands*, refers to it as "completing the action." The survivor tells the story of their trauma *in the body*, often without speaking at all, slowly reconstructing the neural progression of the traumatic experience so that it can reach a conclusion. Shamanic practitioners sometimes call this process one of soul retrieval, and the term feels more accurate to me than any clinical language, which by definition excludes the spiritual nature of healing. The essential nature of self that we recover and transform by healing, by revising and completing the story of the past, is often more completely described by spiritual terms.

The second phase of repentance according to Maimonides is "a relation to the past . . . reform itself is not returning." That is, in order to return, the confessor must tell the story of their wrongs. As for the memoirist and the survivor, for the repentant, "The past recollected is painful, indeed, may make one sorrowful." A return to God requires a return to the past, a reckoning with what is most unresolved in her, and with her own responsibility.

Seven hundred years after Maimonides, another philosopher, Hermann Cohen, writes of confession as the process of "re-cognizing" that the confessor is the maker of his own guilt. Cohen argues for the inadvertent nature of all wrongs, and so it is only upon reflection that agency is taken and complicity understood. As Robert Gibbs explains in his book *Why Ethics?*: "Returning is learning to know yourself again, to find your own agency in the actions that you have committed."

Replace the word *returning* with *writing*, and you have a sentence that could confidently be uttered by anyone who has authored a memoir. "Writing is learning to know yourself again, to find your own agency in the actions that you have committed." It could likewise be revised by any survivor who has reconstructed her story: "*Recovering* is learning to know yourself again, to find your own agency in the actions that have been committed."

Reading Gibbs's words for the first time, I thought of AA's fourth step, when the sober person writes an exhaustive inventory of their resentments, which is, inevitably, also a kind of autobiography. Many newly sober people expect to reflect on their own self-righteousness during this exercise, and many are surprised to find instead a humbling catalog of their own misdeeds.

"Only by re-cognizing my deed as my own can I hope to know myself as the author of my misdeeds" is an explication of Cohen's philosophy, but it might just as easily have been lifted from AA's *Big Book*, which was, like the whole program of the twelve steps, powerfully informed by much older spiritual texts and practices.

In memoir, an honest and awake recollection and retrieval of the past can be similarly enlightening. It is, of course, not always about recognizing, like Cohen's confessor, that we are the maker of our own suffering, though it always includes revelations about the nature of our role in the past. Often, it also yields insights into the roles others played in our story. Sometimes, it even reveals insight about the future.

In the summer of 2014, I spent a month at a residency writing the first draft of the title essay of *Abandon Me*. I was still in the relationship that I was writing about. I

wanted the essay to fill in the gaps left between the previous essays I'd written. After my long days of writing,
I would wander around the wooded property, trying to
find a cell phone signal strong enough to allow me to continue arguing with my lover.

Two years in, and I was still trying to make it work. I
was still committed to the story we were telling: that our
love was true, and that the agony of our dynamic was not
evidence contesting that fact, but proving it. I intended
the essay to articulate this story as a kind of hero's journey, wherein my narrator surmounted the many obsta-
cles on her course to happiness and claimed her trophy
of true love.

By the final week of my stay, I had produced nearly
one hundred pages of an essay that I had intended to be
around forty. I could feel that I was closing in on the final
act of the story, which I knew I could not complete until
I had lived it. Part of my task in the final days of my residency was to make notes toward my expected ending.
My lover was due to move across the country and into
my apartment shortly thereafter—an event which would
mark the culmination my desires over the previous two
years. It would be a perfect happy ending for my essay.

The state of mind that I reach when I am deep in my work is a kind of trance, characterized by total self-forgetting. It is a kind of animal state, singularly focused and unselfconscious. I am inside of an intelligence that is driven by instinct and imagination, that is utterly separate from the mind that *thinks* of emails and to-do lists and how others might see me. It has no allegiance to the story I'm committed to living. It is loyal only to the work to which it is applied. It is in this state that I had the lucid and entirely certain realization that there was only one correct ending to my story: my narrator would leave her lover.

What can I say about the strange manner in which I noted this fact, delivered by my creative intelligence, yet continued my course without interruption? Well, without *perceptible* interruption. That realization was a tear in the fabric of my own delusion that expedited its end. I believe now that I would have left her anyway, that such an ending was inevitable, but if I had not glimpsed my own certainty in the crystal ball of my work, and suffered the cognitive dissonance that followed, it would have taken longer. I have learned from this, and a lifetime of other examples, that I am more loyal to the truth in my writing than I am to the truth in my life. As Adrienne Rich writes: "The unconscious wants truth, as the body does."

This experience was a harbinger not only of the true ending to my book and the end of my relationship, but of the work that would follow. Writing this, I think again of Trethewey's return to the site of her mother's murder. I, too, had thought that I was running away from a confrontation with the truth, but in fact, in writing that book, I had been working my way steadily toward it.

After I lived and then wrote that ending, I had to go back and revise my hero's journey. It was not true love that my hero had been fighting for, but a false story of it. She had been in a kind of bondage, and I first understood this bondage as the work of my lover. But when I revisited the past in my revision, I could see how I had collaborated with her in this project. I had worshipped her like a god both cruel and adoring. I had asked of her what only a god could provide. I had used her the way I had once used heroin and I had become just as powerless over my compulsion. It was only in locating this complicity that I could write a story worth reading. It was only by doing so that I could free myself from the past.

"Confessing makes me know myself," writes Gibbs. "Knowing myself is an act of transforming myself."

I often tell my students about the importance of authorial distance. The *I* of their narrator is not the *I* that writes the book. It is not the complex and fluctuating matrix that makes up their self or their personality or their identity. It is a personification of a single strand of these, the one that occupies their story of the past, which is also a single strand plucked from a larger matrix.

Successful narration of a memoir depends upon the careful interplay of the past *I* and the present—whether it be explicit or implicit in the text. Self-knowledge, the insights unavailable in the past and acquired in the time since, are what give memoir its depth. It is not experience that qualifies a person to write a memoir, but insight into experience, and the ability to tell a story of the past that contains both dimensions. That is, the past experience has been *integrated* into the larger narrative of the author's life. For me, and I believe for most memoirists, the process of writing is also a process of comprehension, an examination of the past that yields new understanding.

There are many other elements of craft that make a work of art, of course, and these, too, have often been mediators in my process of comprehending experience. In those early essays of *Abandon Me*, I did not have access to the cognitive functions that could explicitly make sense of my situation. But through the lyric modes of my work, I could draw upon less conscious forms of sense making. In the end, these portraits helped compose the larger picture of my narrative, thrown into relief by the more lucid accounts I wrote after I ended the relationship and began the more conscious process of retrieving myself.

Cohen, too, is interested in the individual *I*:

> It speaks, making its past known. Not the simple re-cognition of itself, but rather a re-citation of a past that is not itself, but is what it was, when it was ignorant, indeed when it was not. The confessing I is not a recursion of the self with itself (a simple recognition), but a radical return of the self to what it did not know as itself, through the speaking of "I," through the making known of its own relation to the past.

Beginning writers often fear the vulnerability of expos-
ing their most intimate experiences and their past ignorance in published work. It is important to remember
that most of us write our books alone. Memoirs begin as
conversations with the self. Our first confessions must be
to this internal witness. I test words for the unspoken in
the privacy of the page for as long as I need to before another set of eyes ever sees it. By the time most books find
their unknown readers, the transformation has already
occurred. The writer's relationship to the past is irrevo-
cably changed. The writer is changed.

"To become anew, the old must not be . . . only recognized, but made known as now decisively past. The
returner confesses that he is no longer what he was.
He makes the past known in order to know himself as
changed."

*You make the past known in order to know yourself as
changed.*

However, as the confessor cannot re-cognize her past
without the knowledge of a loving god, nor the survivor
construct and mourn the story of her trauma without
a trusted witness, the writer cannot complete her story
without a conception of a loving audience. Despite all our
worries about reception, perhaps no book is completed

without a belief in a perfect reader, the person who most needs our story.

For this reason, I have related as much to Montaigne as Augustine. "As for me," the famous essayist writes, "I may desire in a general way to be different; I may . . . implore God to reform me completely and to pardon my natural weakness. But this I ought not to call repentance." It is acceptance, rather, that is most transformative to the essayist. As John D. Sykes Jr. writes in *God and Self in the Confessional Novel*: "However strange Montaigne may appear to himself, he hopes by his honesty . . . to identify himself in the eyes of the reader with a general humanity, so that he and the reader are united in a bond of solidarity . . . And in this way, he solves the puzzle of himself and comes to self-acceptance."

4.

The third phase of repentance is the act of confession. While the first two phases happen solely in the self, confession calls for a witness. God has known the sinner's truth all along, has loved and accepted her without flaw, "but cannot witness the return until the returner calls for God to witness."

Here is how I understand it: the confessor has always

been loved, but cannot be reassured of this until she confesses.

I know so intimately how it feels to be loved and have not confessed. Remember Winnicott: "It is joy to be hidden and disaster not to be found." This part is of the disaster. A secret is anathema to believing love is true, a kernel of promise that if the past is exposed, love will abandon her.

What a terrible predicament: to not know if love is conditional and yet to understand that the only way to find out is to risk losing it. I don't know where everyone who takes that risk finds their faith, but I know where I have found it: first on the page, where I test those early words, groping for a way to say what I have tried to hide and hide from. Then, in the freedom I have found by being seen. Not by the reader, but by my own higher power, by the self that is capable of holding the most pitiful part of my past and loving her clean. I need *the idea* of audience for this, but the first witness is never a stranger.

In an interview just after my first book was published, I remember quipping about my adolescence that "I was busy getting finger-banged behind the mall." I cringe now, to even type these words. Not because they are crude, but because they are cruel. Because they evidence such ignorance. I had thought them witty at the time, albeit in a hard sort of way. The hardness was partly the point. Embedded in that choice was my abiding belief in the fantasy of toughness—the idea that lack of feeling signified mastery of it. It is true that there is a kind of social power in the pageantry of uncaring. It renders one less vulnerable to others. That protection can exact a steep price. I have since come to understand much greater powers.

The twelve-year-old who had been finger-banged behind the mall was the same girl who had been spat upon by the neighbor she adored. Her body had developed early and she was in the midst of a year characterized by relentless sexual harassment at school, and the shocking change of her body's meaning in the world—a confounding degradation publicized as a promotion. Her own desire combined with social conditioning made it impossible to deflect or refuse every sexual petition. She did not enjoy being finger-banged behind the mall. She had only wanted to be kissed. She had followed the call of her own desire and unknowingly entered into a contract that promised more than she wanted to give.

In light of these facts, my quip to the interviewer seems spectacularly mean. But time and experience have softened me even to the instinct that prompted it. It was only my early attempt to manage the pain of that time, the bouquet of traumas that were not mitigated by their ordinariness and from which I had moved on but not truly recovered. By refusing to acknowledge their traumatic nature, I had been unable to integrate them fully.

It was only in writing the essays of *Girlhood* that I faced that story directly—the harassment, the many sexual experiences during which I felt like a ghost of myself, the estrangement from my loving parents, my inability to reconcile the sudden degradation of being a female-bodied person in the world—and the many ways its symptoms had played out in the years since, perpetuating their harm as imperceptibly as a crude, throwaway remark in an interview.

I could not have written that book without the many good therapists I've seen. I also could not have written it without believing in the reader who needed it. At the outset of the process, before I could muster much tenderness for my young self, I could love that invisible reader. I could feel her love in return. And as I wrote, her figure expanded and contracted until it matched the shape of my young heroine.

"In confession, one promises, before God, never to turn away again . . . Speaking itself seals the future, testifies against myself—binding me to not return to sin."

This articulation of Gibbs's reminds me of the often misquoted words of another philosopher, George Santayana, who wrote that "those who cannot remember the past are condemned to repeat it." Perhaps it can also be said that those who cannot *speak* (or write) of the past are condemned to regret it.

Confession is not only a cognitive act, though it is that. Franz Rosenzweig, another Jewish philosopher, writes: "The soul speaks, I have sinned, and does away with shame. In so speaking purely back into the past, it cleanses the present from the weakness of the past."

I have rarely written of anything that did not carry some shame. As a writer, I trade almost exclusively in topics that I once believed unspeakable, that were unspoken. The urge to write them was as fervent as my urge to confess as a child, as the exquisite yearning I feel in response to certain kinds of music. I believe their impetus is the same: to speak and be seen, to confirm that I am lovable.

When I say that I have no regrets, it might sound arrogant. What I mean is that I have returned to the parts of my past that pained me and uncovered the aspects that I most wanted to avoid. I have grieved and I have taken responsibility. I have revised the story of my victimhood and my culpability. I have completed what was interrupted, what stuttered like a skipping record for decades. I have brought to it my questions, like some oracle, made myself a supplicant to the past, asked her what I could not when I was her, and told her what she could not tell herself. Through this process, I have become able to love her. I have done it all in writing, and that "performance of confessing," as Gibbs explains, "has led to confessing being BELOVED."

The final phase of trauma recovery is often described as grounded in a reconnection and restored engagement with social life. The survivor has completed the narrative of her trauma, in body and mind, has regained some ability to trust, has undone the binds of shame. She is ready to step back into public view.

Often, this stage of recovery includes the realization that the survivor, as Judith Herman writes, "can transform the meaning of their personal tragedy by making it the basis for social action." The survivor shares her experience publicly by becoming a lecturer or spokesperson, an activist, a person who tells the story of her assault on social media followed by the hashtag #MeToo.

"Survivors undertake to speak about the unspeakable in public in the belief that this will help others," Herman elaborates. "In doing so, they feel connected to a power larger than themselves." That is, like the confessor, they perform another kind of return.

As memoirists, we, too, speak about the unspeakable in public in the belief that this will help others. While I know that the person helped most of all is myself, part of my own healing has come from the hundreds of strangers who have written to me, claiming that I told their story, too, and that reading it showed them that it was possible to tell.

The literature on trauma widely addresses the importance of commonality to the survivor's recovery. So agreed upon is the healing power of shared experience that almost every form of trauma survivor can easily find a group of similar survivors with whom to bond and find mutual support.

Similarly, twelve-step programs insist that one of the essential ingredients in their effectiveness is the trust engendered by the shared nature of the recovering addicts' experiences. That is, I could never speak of my most humiliating experiences—the things that brought me to my knees and for which I crawled—without believing there was someone who truly understood on the other end of my words.

After I had completed the personal portions of *Girlhood*, revisited the past, and redefined my relationship to that twelve-year-old girl, I began speaking to other women about their experiences of adolescent sexual harassment, empty consent, and the repercussions of those in the years that followed.[17] I was not shocked by the similarities in our stories, but they made a very deep impression. There was a degree of catharsis, of relief after those conversations that was different than any the writing alone had induced.

Those women were the first people to whom I'd

literally spoken of these experiences, and they'd broken their own silences in return. I don't know that I could call up all their names from memory right now, but in those intimate conversations, we came to love each other in a specific way that depends upon the trust of shared experience. The experience sealed the future, served as a testimony against my past relationship to those events. They *cured* me, in both senses of the word, and they prepared me for that more visible outward turning, toward an audience who had only existed thus far in theory.

Part of what ultimately and most conclusively resolves trauma is the recognizable public acknowledgment of it. Think of war monuments, or military awards for those injured in combat. Our society has been much quicker to acknowledge the traumas typically suffered by men. Rape victims do not get monuments in public spaces. They rarely even get legal justice.

In addition to the satisfaction of transforming her pain into something useful to others and connecting her to a power greater than herself, the social change a trauma survivor manifests can serve as a kind of monument.

A memoir is also a kind of monument, as the title of

Trethewey's memoir, *Memorial Drive*, hints. A public manifestation of the writer's story, like any monument, it can carry tremendous political power. It can carry spiritual power. It is the proof not only that we have survived, that it is possible to survive such experiences, but that we can integrate them into our lives in ways that empower us, that make us more resilient and wise and connected— to ourselves, to others like us, and to all kinds of higher powers.

"This is how the past fits into the narrative of our lives, gives meaning and purpose," writes Trethewey. "Even my mother's death is redeemed in the story of my calling, made meaningful rather than senseless."

5.

There was a pop song a few years ago that played on the radio frequently. After teaching a night class, I would be too exhausted to listen to podcasts or the dreadful news and I'd scan the radio. It got so that I'd always stop for this song. It was a love song, and a kind of hymn. It was, of course, a beggin'-ass song. *The only Heaven I'll be sent to / is when I'm alone with you,* the singer claims. *I was born sick, but I love it / Command me to be well / A-, Amen, Amen, Amen.*

The song wrenched something in me so pure and hungry, it was a pleasure close to agony, near erotic. I felt it in my *body*. I was not in love at the time, but when I listened to that song I felt like I was. The words evoke this as much as the music, the language of supplication, the plaintive call of the worshipful. It was the same feeling I'd known as a girl, the same I'd known in love, the same I'd felt in response to so many other songs. As I drove down the night highway, my heart surged and surged. I was, of course, on the brink of writing something that scared me.

I have worshipped people the way that others worship gods, have looked to humans and chemicals for the kind of love we can only expect from a divine source. Our culture encourages this. We think love will redeem us, and it will, but not that of any human lover and not that of any material substance. I have found a church in art, a form of work that is also a form of worship—it is a means of understanding myself, all my past selves, and all of you as beloved.

This is why I will never stop doing it, even if no publisher ever again wants to share the results. Ironically, this kind of investment in the process is a boon to those who seek publication. Tenacity is often cited as the most common characteristic of successful authors. Of the many talented people I've met—classmates, students, friends—many of them no longer write.[18] The ones who have kept doing so have made it central to their lives both external and internal. Writing is hard. It is not the most apparently useful kind of work to do in the world. Most of us are not out here saving any lives but our own, though its power to do that (at least in my case) is uncontestable. The older I get, the less convinced I am about most things, but this is one of the great facts of my life.

I cannot imagine nurturing a devotion to any practice more consistently than one which yields the reward of transformation, the assurance of lovability, and the eradication of regret. No professional ambition could possibly matter more than the freedom to return, again and again.

These are not perfect analogies. I don't mean to claim that they are. My primary argument is that whatever the contemporary associations with memoir or personal narrative or confession or the therapeutic elements of making art, when we write this way we are performing a process that predates those biases by centuries. I have felt its pull as far back as memory goes, and I believe that it goes back much, much further than that.

There are geometric shapes that recur in nature, the shapes on which it is most possible to build, known by carpenters and tides and insects alike. We, too—in our rituals of healing, creation, and repentance—are performing a pattern that has recurred at the center of human life as far back as it is recorded. Why should our idea of intrinsic nature be confined to the biological, and who says that the spiritual, the creative, and the psychological do not manifest biologically? We know that they do.

Delineating the process of human transformation in psychological or spiritual terms are often two ways of describing the same process. These are just models for understanding, invented by humans. They aren't the only ones I could use.[19] The spiral does not *belong* to the nautilus shell, unless it also belongs to the whirlpool, the hurricane, the galaxy, the double helix of DNA, the tendrils of a common vine. If there are golden ratios that govern the structures of our bodies and our world, then

of course there must be such shapes among the less mea-
surable aspects of existence.

As a child, I did not understand spiritual, cathartic,
and aesthetic processes as discrete and I still don't. It is
through writing that I have come to know that for me
they are inextricable. I am much more interested in what
art is and can be than in what it is not. It is a form of
worship, a medicine, a solitary and a social act. It is an
ancient process through which I draw closer to my ances-
tors. On the page, I undergo a change of heart, I return
to the past and make something new from it, I forgive
myself and am freed from old harms, I return to love and
am blessed with more than enough to give away. Every
single thing I have created worth a damn has been a practice of love, healing, and redemption. I know this process
to be divine.

Acknowledgments

An earlier version of "In Praise of Navel-Gazing" was published in the January/February 2017 issue of *Poets & Writers*.

"Mind Fuck: Writing Better Sex" began as a craft lecture written for and delivered at the Tin House Summer Workshop, and an earlier version of the resultant essay was published in the Summer 2020 issue of *The Sewanee Review*.

Big thanks to Jonathan Lee, Megha Majumdar, Megan Fishmann, Alisha Gorder, Rachel Fershleiser, Nicole Caputo, Jordan Koluch, and everyone at Catapult. Also my agent, Ethan Bassoff, who donated his commission to support a fellowship to Lambda Literary's retreat for emerging LGBTQI writers. I was only able to finish writing this book due to a residency at MacDowell, a place that has been a home for so much of my best work.

Many of the ideas, arguments, and insights in this book began first as conversations—with friends, students, mentors, and most often by far, my brilliant wife, Donika Kelly, whose love, intelligence, and curiosity nourishes everything I write. Nika, you make everything more interesting—let's keep the conversation going for a big long time.

Notes

1. Interestingly, Aristotle used the word *catharsis* solely to refer to the release of menstrual fluids until he adopted it as a metaphor in *Poetics.*

2. It is an appropriate response to so many unwelcome comments:

    "You should smile more, beautiful!"

    "My sexuality has been the single most powerful disruptive force mankind has ever perceived, and its repression has been the work of centuries."

    "Are you sure you want to eat that?"

    "My sexuality has been the single most powerful disruptive force mankind has ever perceived, and its repression has been the work of centuries."

"C'mon just the tip!"

"My sexuality has been the single most powerful disruptive force mankind has ever perceived, and its repression has been the work of centuries."

3. I won't elaborate here, partly out of a desire to protect my own privacy, partly out of a desire to protect my ability to enjoy watching these sorts of porn, which, if subjected to articulation and more direct analysis, might be ruined for pleasure.

4. It's not a booming industry *per se*, but there are definitely options for the queer feminist masturbator who wants to see videos of real queer women fucking each other and possibly even having real orgasms.

5. I actually went to my bookshelves in search of some examples of these and then remembered a recent purge in which I donated all the ones that came most quickly to mind (see partial list in the subsequent note). I didn't feel moved enough to go digging online for the examples of which I had purged my home. The ones that remained on my shelves are more contemporary and because I have already been exhausted by the public conversation about their misdeeds and the subsequent connections to their work, I don't want to distract with more specificity. Some I keep, because

there is so much else to love about their work. Others
I can let go of because there are plenty of other good
books.

6. Hesse, Bukowski, Kerouac, Miller, Hemingway,
Mailer, et al.

7. "Let's, for a moment, take the whole spectrum of
sexual violence—the emotional abuse, exploitation,
and sexual abuse of children; family molestation;
stranger and date rape; the paltry sentencing laws;
the acute vulnerability of indigenous women, women
of color, and transgender communities; rape culture;
the degrading humiliations war brings; and the ongoing dangers and indignities refugees suffer—let's
take it all and lump it together under one encompass-
ing term: rapism."

8. In one of my creative writing workshops during un-
dergrad, a classmate brought in a short story with
a scene of graphic coercive sex. A few years later, I
would have known to call it rape. I would have been
able to say that in the class. But instead, I listened to
our teacher talk about how hard "sex scenes" are to
write.

9. Or, that it's never effective to describe them as such.
See Michael Cunningham's 2010 novel *By Nightfall*,

which contains one of the best longtime-married sex scenes I've ever read and includes the description: "Her nipples may have thickened and darkened a little—they are now precisely the size of the tip of his little finger, and the color of pencil erasers. Were they once slightly smaller, a little pinker? Probably. He is actually one of the few men who doesn't obsess about younger women, which she refuses to believe.

"We always worry about the wrong things, don't we?"

10. It does seem important to note that multiple studies over the past few decades, including one in 2018, show that queer women overall have more orgasms than straight women and are more likely to "receive more oral sex, have longer duration of last sex, be more satisfied with their relationship, ask for what they want in bed, praise their partner for something they did in bed, call/email to tease about doing something sexual, wear sexy lingerie, try new sexual positions, anal stimulation, act out fantasies, incorporate sexy talk, and express love during sex."

11. This alleged letter to Tallulah Bankhead from Billie Holiday has been replicated in many places, but I could not find a primary source, though their

relationship has been written about in significant detail by the biographers of each woman.

12. The incomparable Mary Karr wrote of memoirs (in *The Art of Memoir*) that "nobody I know who's written a great one described it as anything less than a major-league shit-eating contest." I tend to agree. Writing a memoir about how writing one's memoirs pissed people off would be a kind of infinite hall of mirrors depicting various shit-eating contests. No thank you.

13. This was circa 2004–05, in the early days of Bushwick's gentrification, when it was still mostly artists and musicians who were invading the industrial corners of the primarily Latinx neighborhood, before the gleaming condo buildings began to spring up. Our decrepit building's hallways perpetually billowed with weed smoke, their floors often littered with broken glass. Once, a pile of shit sat on a stairwell landing for a full day, unclear to all whether its source was human or canine.

14. I have already written at length about my experiences with my father and this subject, in the essay "Girl at a Window" in *Abandon Me*. I considered reiterating them here, but found that I had no interest in doing

so—once I have plumbed a vulnerable subject to its depth, subsequent reiterations feel lifeless. Also, most of the wisdom gleaned from those experiences has been expressed in the stories I have shared.

15. It is important to clarify that the genre of the romantic mad lady writer is largely a white genre, and it was my whiteness that granted me access to this romantic packaging of my sadness. Margo Jefferson writes in *Negroland* that as a Black woman she was "denied the privilege of freely yielding to depression, of flaunting neurosis as a mark of social and psychic complexity. A privilege that was glorified in the literature of white female suffering and resistance."

16. Peter Levine describes in *Waking the Tiger* how oftentimes the only way to diagnose whether a trauma has taken place is by accounting for the reliable symptoms. For most of my life, I resisted the evidence that I had undergone trauma because my own conception of it was so narrow. When I finally wrote about my girlhood, it quickly became clear that it was, like most, a comprehensive series of traumas that had been disguised by their commonness. Being female in patriarchy, like being Black, Indigenous, AAPI, or any POC identity in a white supremacist,

colonized nation like ours, is to intimately know myriad forms of trauma related to that systemic oppression throughout the course of our whole lives.

17. *Empty consent* is a term that I invented while writing *Girlhood* that refers to affirmative consent given despite internal ambivalence, aversion, or revulsion.

18. Mary Oliver wrote that "the most regretful people on earth are those who felt the call to creative work, who felt their own creative power restive and uprising, and gave to it neither power nor time." I seriously doubt that this is true, though the regret of such people does seem persistent and long-standing.

19. An earlier draft of this essay included the analogous nature of narrative design.

Sources Consulted and Further Reading

In Praise of Navel-Gazing

Aretaeus of Cappadocia. *Aretaiou Kappadokou Ta sozomena = The extant works of Aretaeus, the Cappadocian.* Translated and edited by Francis Adams. London: Sydenham Society, 1856.

Belfiore, Elizabeth S. *Tragic Pleasures: Aristotle on Plot and Emotion.* Princeton, NJ: Princeton University Press, 1992.

Centers for Disease Control and Prevention. "Preventing Sexual Violence." Updated February 5, 2021. www.cdc.gov/violenceprevention/sexualviolence/fastfact.html.

Freud, Sigmund, and Josef Breuer. *Studies in Hysteria.*

Translated by Nicola Luckhurst. New York: Penguin Classics, 2004.

Gass, William H. "The art of self." *Harper's Magazine,* May 1994.

Herman, Judith. *Trauma and Recovery: The Aftermath of Violence—from Domestic Abuse to Political Terror.* New York: Basic Books, 1997.

Million, Dian. "Felt Theory: An Indigenous Feminist Approach to Affect and History." *Wicazo Sa Review* 24, no. 2 (Fall 2009): 53–76.

Nelson, Maggie. *The Argonauts.* Minneapolis, MN: Graywolf Press, 2016.

Pennebaker, James W. "Writing About Emotional Experiences as a Therapeutic Process." *Psychological Science* 8, no. 3 (May 1997): 162–166.

Pennebaker, James W., Dario Paez, and Bernard Rimé, eds. *Collective Memory of Political Events.* New York: Psychology Press, 1997.

Rilke, Rainer Maria. *Letters to a Young Poet.* Translated by M. D. Herter Norton. New York: W. W. Norton & Company, 1993.

Washuta, Elissa. "White Witchery." *Guernica.* February 14, 2019. www.guernicamag.com/white-witchery.

Mind Fuck

Carson, Anne. *Autobiography of Red*. New York: Vintage Contemporaries, 1998.

Cunningham, Michael. *By Nightfall*. New York: Farrar, Straus and Giroux, 2010.

Foucault, Michel. *Discipline and Punish: The Birth of the Prison*. New York: Vintage Books, 1995.

Frederick, David A., H. Kate St. John, Justin R. Garcia, and Elisabeth A. Lloyd. "Differences in Orgasm Frequency Among Gay, Lesbian, Bisexual, and Heterosexual Men and Women in a U.S. National Sample." *Archives of Sexual Behavior* 47, no. 1 (February 2017): 273–288.

Greenwell, Garth. *Cleanness*. New York: Farrar, Straus and Giroux, 2020.

Howe, Marie. *What the Living Do*. New York: W. W. Norton & Company, 1999.

Leilani, Raven. *Luster*. New York: Farrar, Straus and Giroux, 2020.

Lorde, Audre. *Sister Outsider*. Berkeley, CA: Crossing Press, 2007.

Machado, Carmen Maria. "The Trash Heap Has Spoken." *Guernica*. February 13, 2017. www.guernicamag.com/the-trash-heap-has-spoken.

Mairs, Nancy. *Plaintext: Essays.* Tucson, AZ: University of Arizona Press, 1992.

Muscio, Inga. *Cunt: A Declaration of Independence.* 20th Anniversary Edition. New York: Seal Press, 2018.

Myles, Eileen. *Inferno: A Poet's Novel.* New York: OR Books, 2016.

Sontag, Susan. *Styles of Radical Will.* New York: Penguin Classics, 2009.

Strayed, Cheryl. "The Love of My Life." *The Sun*, September 2002.

A Big Shitty Party

Beattie, Melody. *Codependent No More: How to Stop Controlling Others and Start Caring for Yourself.* Center City, MN: Hazelden, 1986.

Castro, Joy. *Family Trouble: Memoirists on the Hazards and Rewards of Revealing Family.* Lincoln, NE: University of Nebraska Press, 2013.

Cohen, Kerry. *The Truth of Memoir: How to Write About Yourself and Others with Honesty, Emotion, and Integrity.* New York: Writer's Digest Books, 2014.

Doty, Mark. "Return to Sender." *The Writer's Chronicle*, October/November 2005.

Karr, Mary. *The Art of Memoir*. New York: Harper Perennial, 2016.

Sedaris, David. "Repeat After Me." In *Dress Your Family in Corduroy and Denim*, 141–156. New York: Little, Brown and Company, 2004.

Tisdale, Sallie. "Violation." In *Violation: Collected Essays*. Portland, OR: Hawthorne Books, 2016.

The Return

Alcoholics Anonymous. 4th Edition. New York: Alcoholics Anonymous World Services, Inc., 2001.

Carroll, Robert, and Stephen Prickett, eds. *The Bible: Authorized King James Version*. New York: Oxford University Press, 2008.

Castro, Joy. *Island of Bones*. Lincoln, NE: University of Nebraska Press, 2012.

Cvetkovich, Ann. *An Archive of Feelings*. Durham, NC: Duke University Press, 2003.

Freud, Sigmund, and Josef Breuer. *Studies in Hysteria*. Translated by Nicola Luckhurst. New York: Penguin Classics, 2004.

Gibbs, Robert. *Why Ethics? Signs of Responsibilities*. Princeton, NJ: Princeton University Press, 2000.

Herman, Judith. *Trauma and Recovery: The Aftermath of Violence—from Domestic Abuse to Political Terror.* New York: Basic Books, 1997.

Hozier. "Take Me to Church." *Hozier.* Island Records, 2014.

James, William. *The Varieties of Religious Experience.* New York: Penguin Classics, 1982.

Jefferson, Margo. *Negroland.* New York: Vintage, 2016.

King, Juliet L. *Art Therapy, Trauma and Neuroscience: Theoretical and Practical Perspectives.* 1st Edition. New York: Routledge, 2016.

Levine, Peter A. *Waking the Tiger: Healing Trauma.* Berkeley, CA: North Atlantic Books, 1997.

Maimonides. *Mishneh Torah.* Rome: Shlomo Ben Yehuda and Ovadia Ben Moshe, c. 1480.

Menakem, Resmaa. *My Grandmother's Hands: Racialized Trauma and the Pathway to Mending Our Hearts and Bodies.* Las Vegas: Central Recovery Press, 2017.

Pennebaker, James W., Dario Paez, and Bernard Rimé, eds. *Collective Memory of Political Events.* New York: Psychology Press, 1997.

Rich, Adrienne. "Women and Honor: Some Notes on Lying." In *On Lies, Secrets, and Silence: Selected Prose*

1966–1978, 185–194. New York: W. W. Norton & Company, 1995.

Sykes, John D., Jr. *God and Self in the Confessional Novel.* London: Palgrave Macmillan, 2018.

Trethewey, Natasha. *Memorial Drive: A Daughter's Memoir.* New York: Ecco, 2020.

MELISSA FEBOS is the author of the critically acclaimed memoir *Whip Smart* and two essay collections: *Abandon Me*, a Lambda Literary Award finalist and Publishing Triangle Award finalist, and *Girlhood*, a national bestseller. The inaugural winner of the Jeanne Córdova Prize for Lesbian/Queer Nonfiction from Lambda Literary and a four-time MacDowell fellow, she is also the recipient of fellowships from Bread Loaf, Lower Manhattan Cultural Council, the BAU Institute at the Camargo Foundation, Vermont Studio Center, the Barbara Deming Memorial Fund, and other organizations. Her essays have appeared in *The Paris Review*, *The Believer*, *McSweeney's Quarterly*, *Granta*, *Tin House*, *The Sun*, *The New York Times Magazine*, and elsewhere. She is an associate professor at the University of Iowa, where she teaches in the nonfiction writing program.